Beach Cottages

Find the Difference Brain Teaser Puzzle Adult Coloring Book

By Beth Ingrias

Want to color more for FREE?

Get a FREE 25 page adult coloring book

visit

www.BethIngrias.com

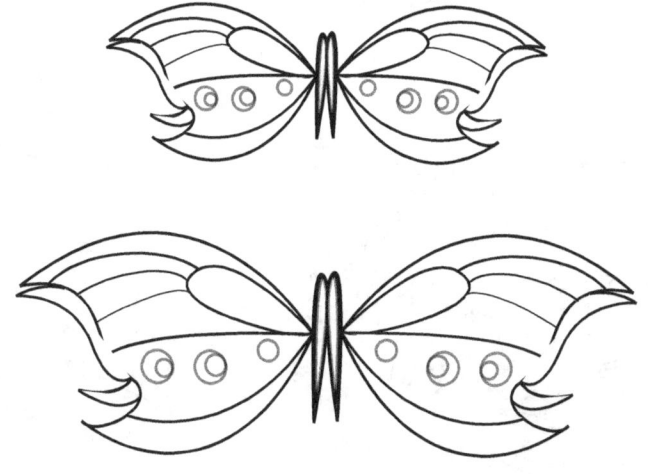

ISBN-13: 978-1-945803-18-5
ISBN-10: 1-945803-18-5

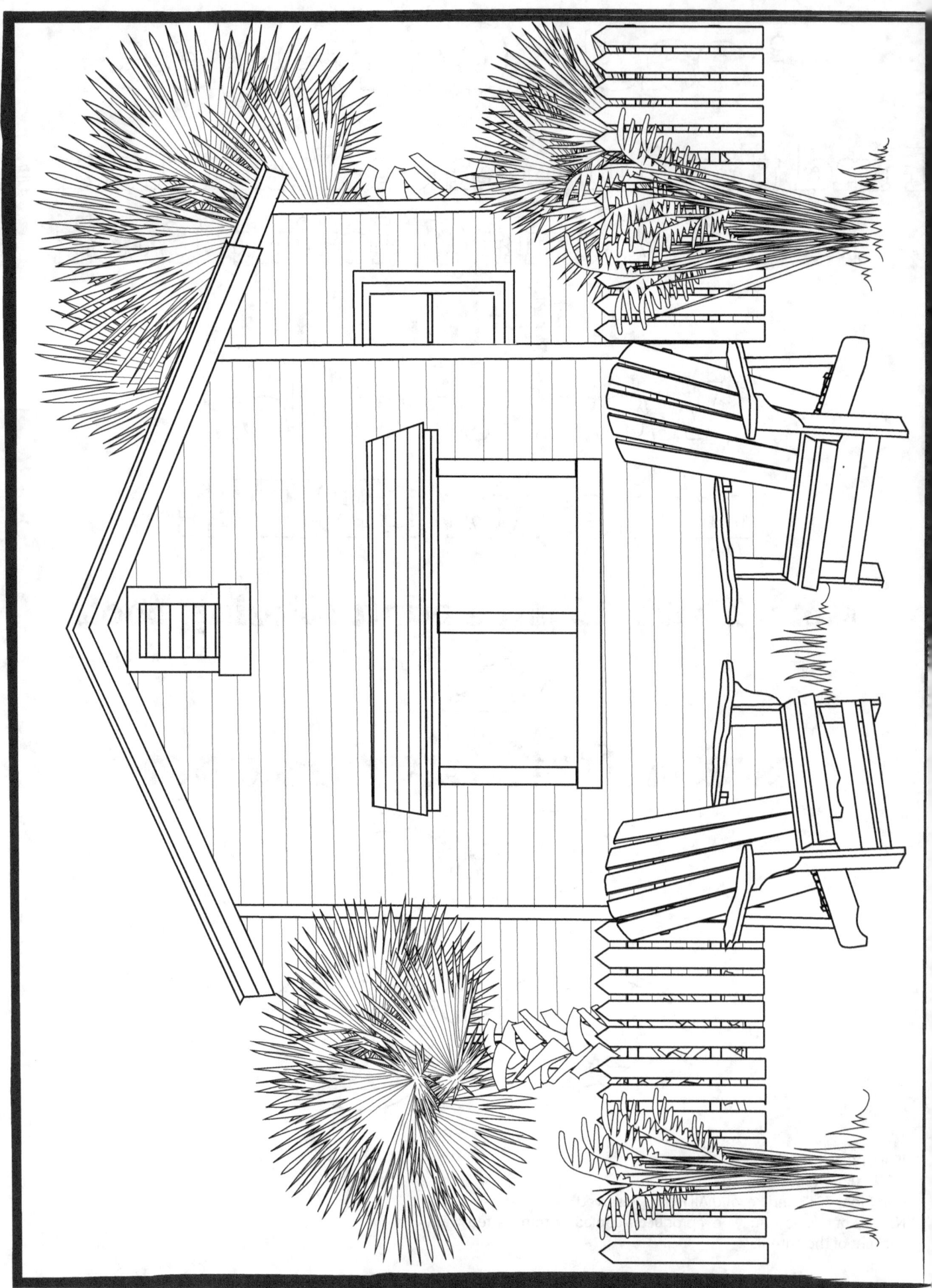

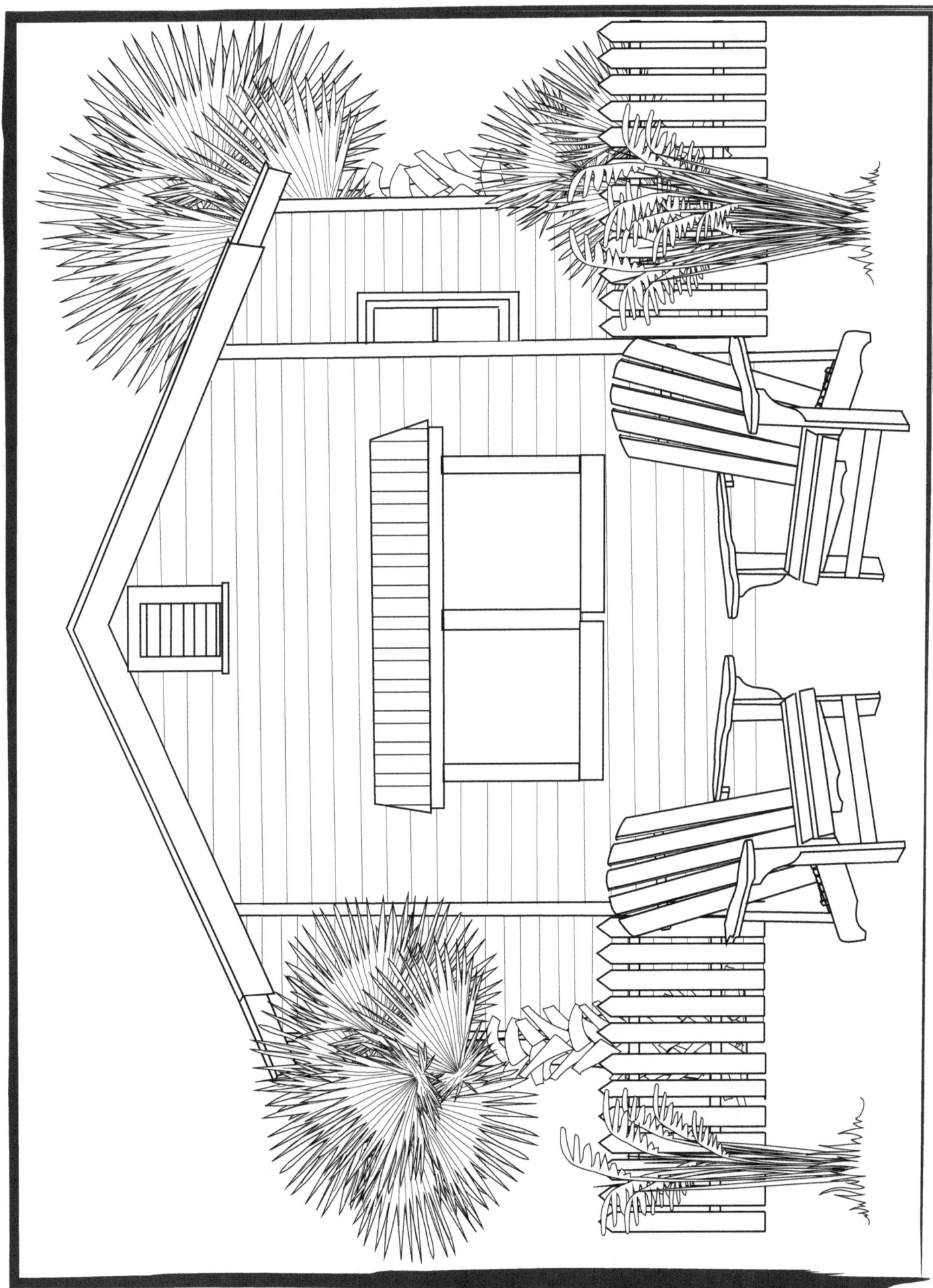

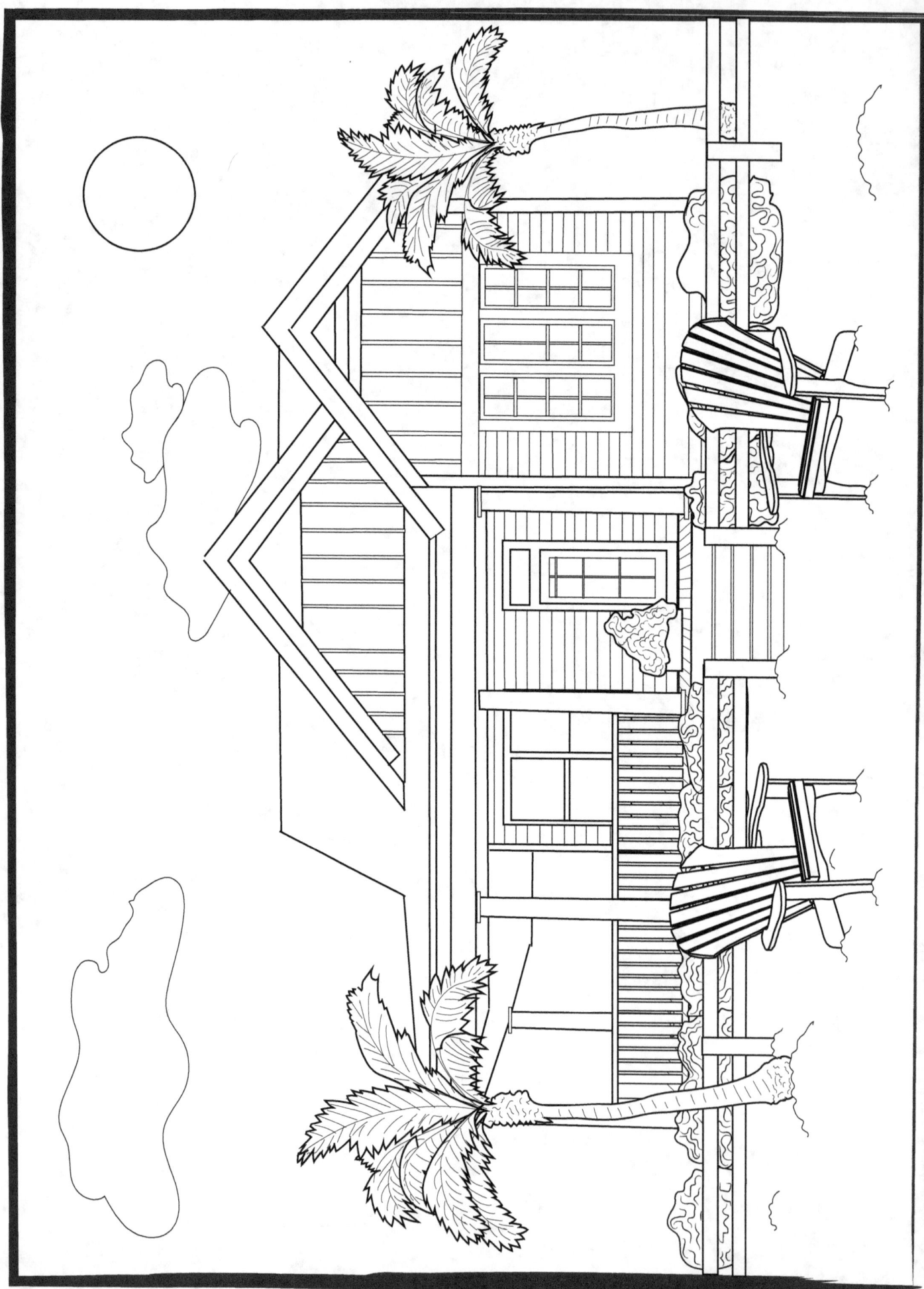

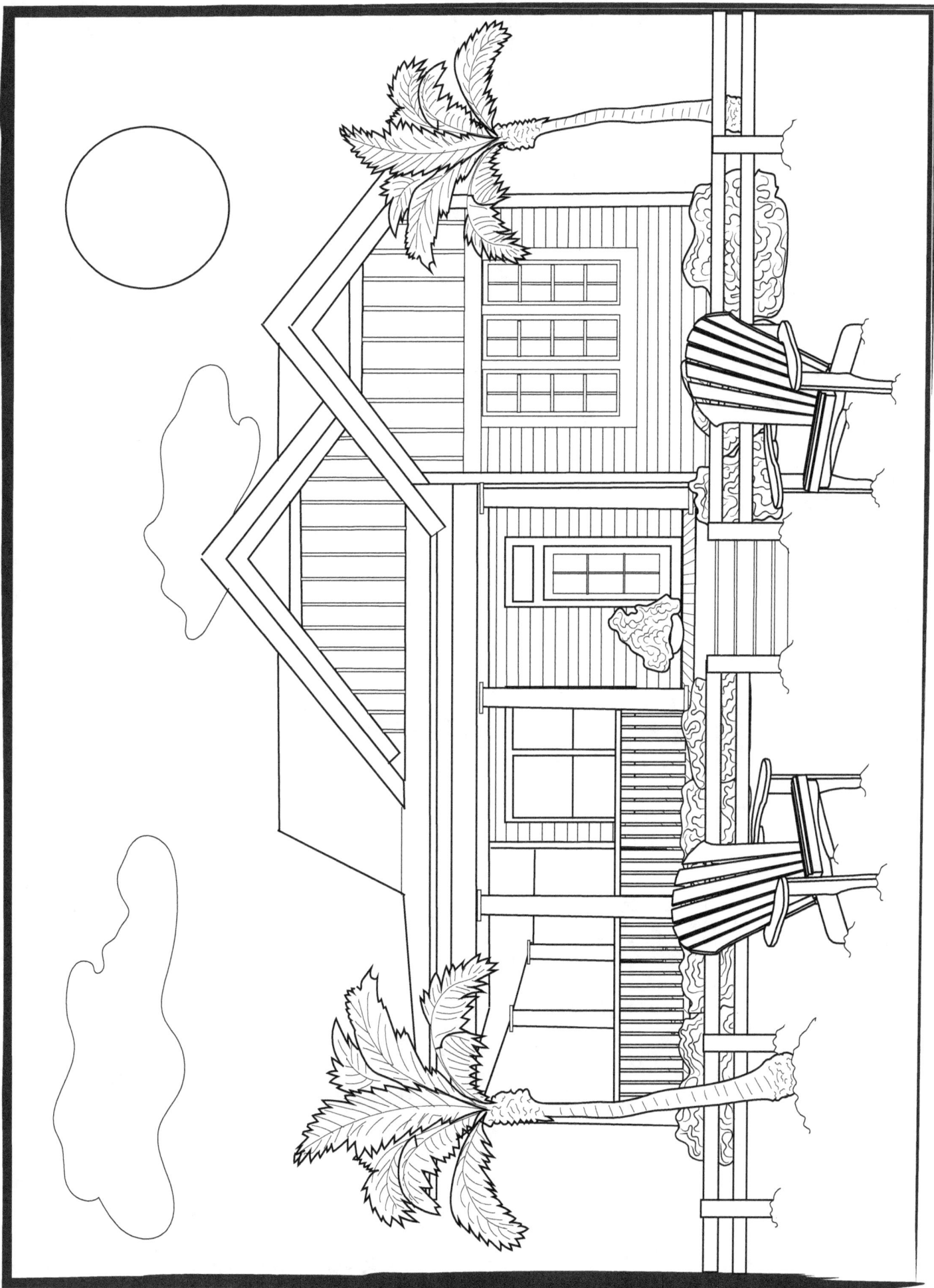

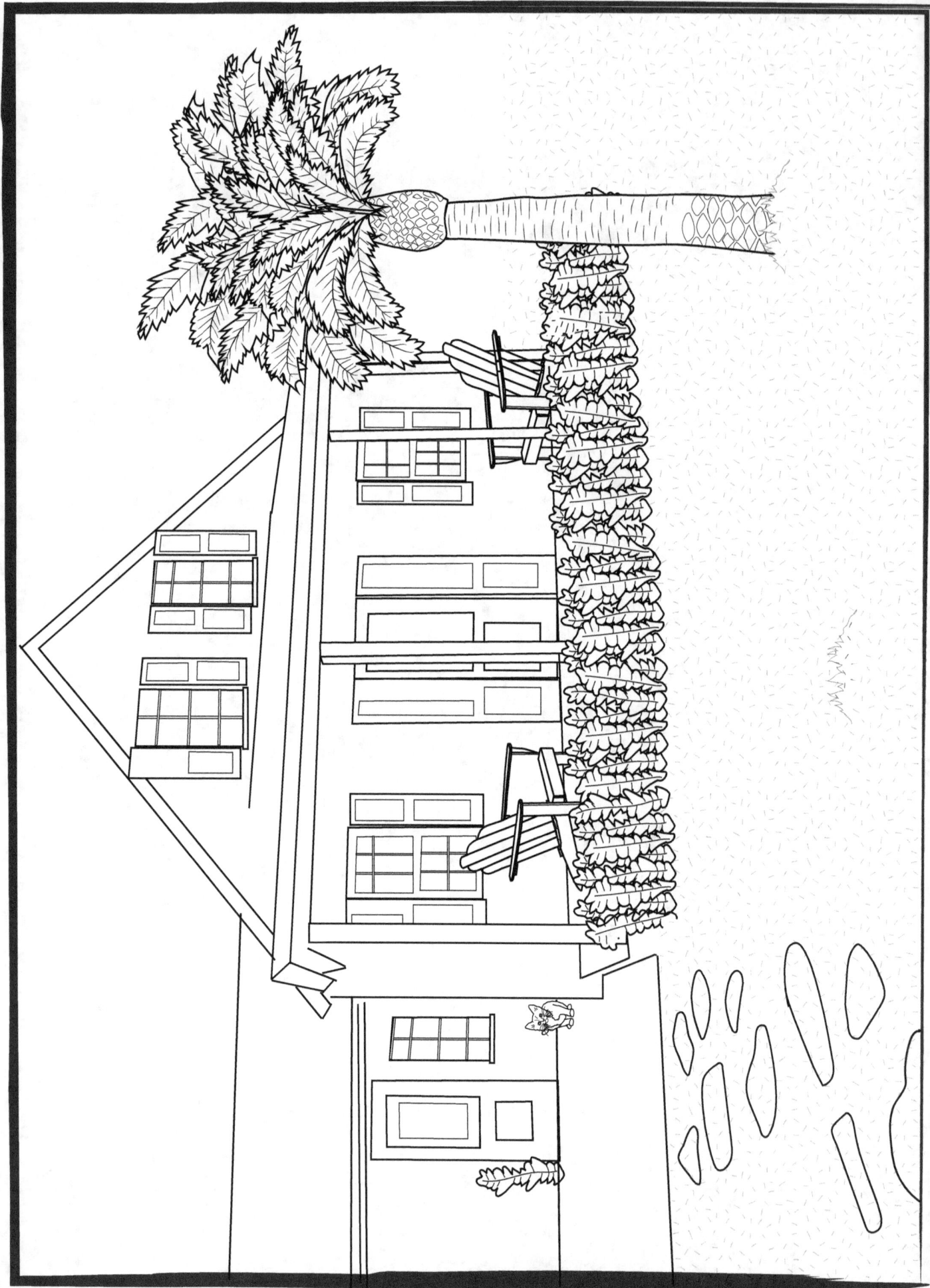

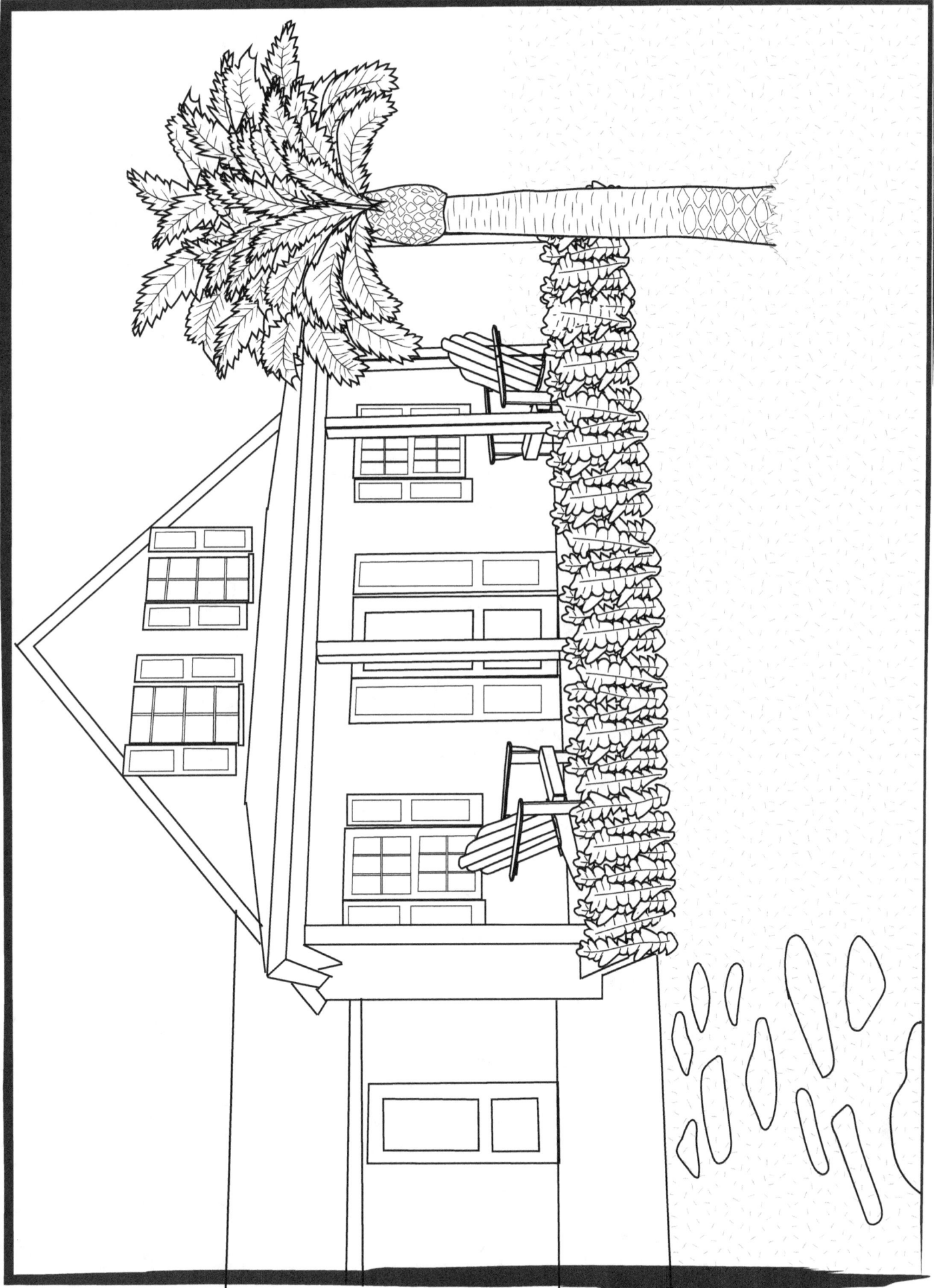

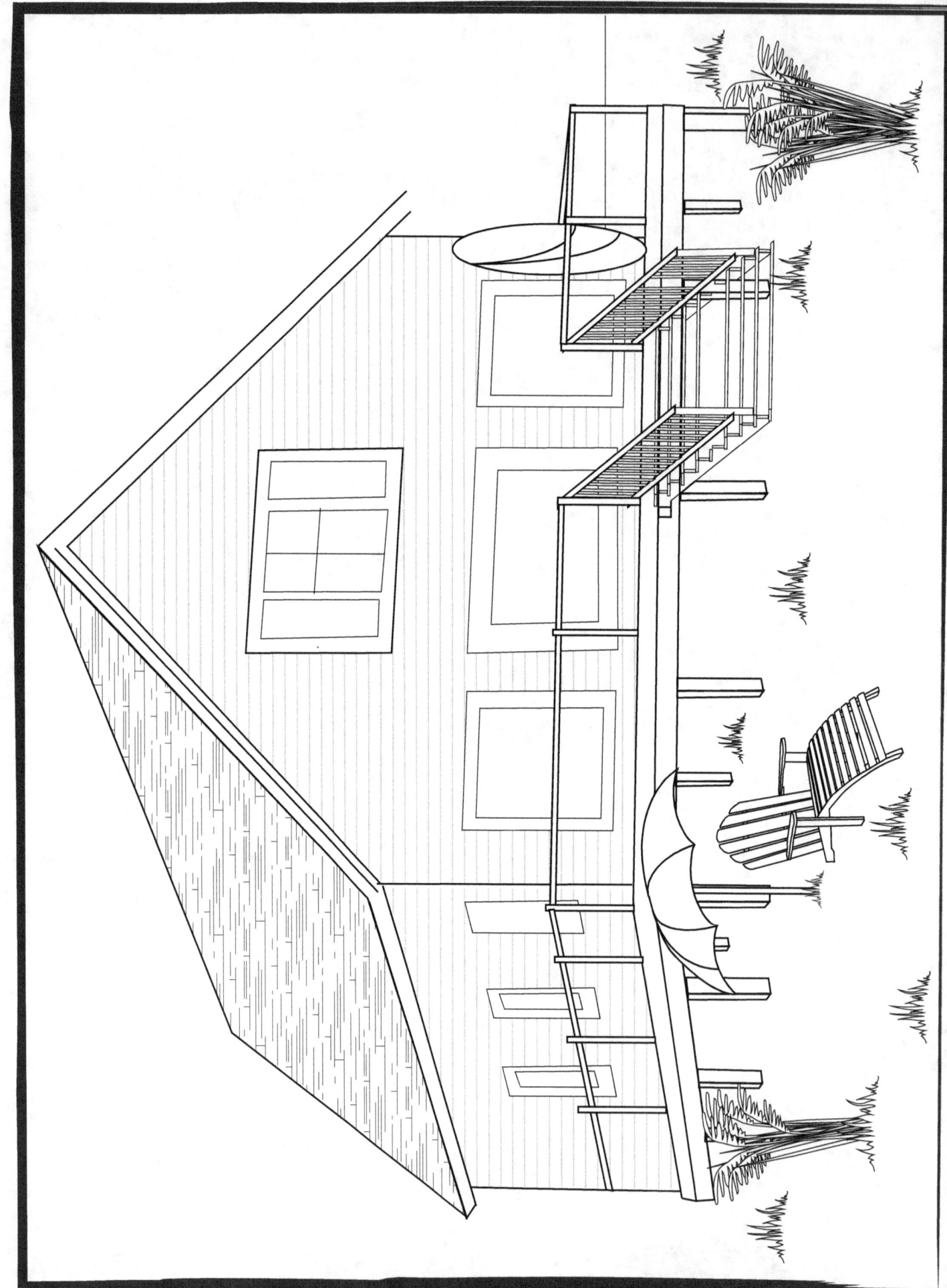

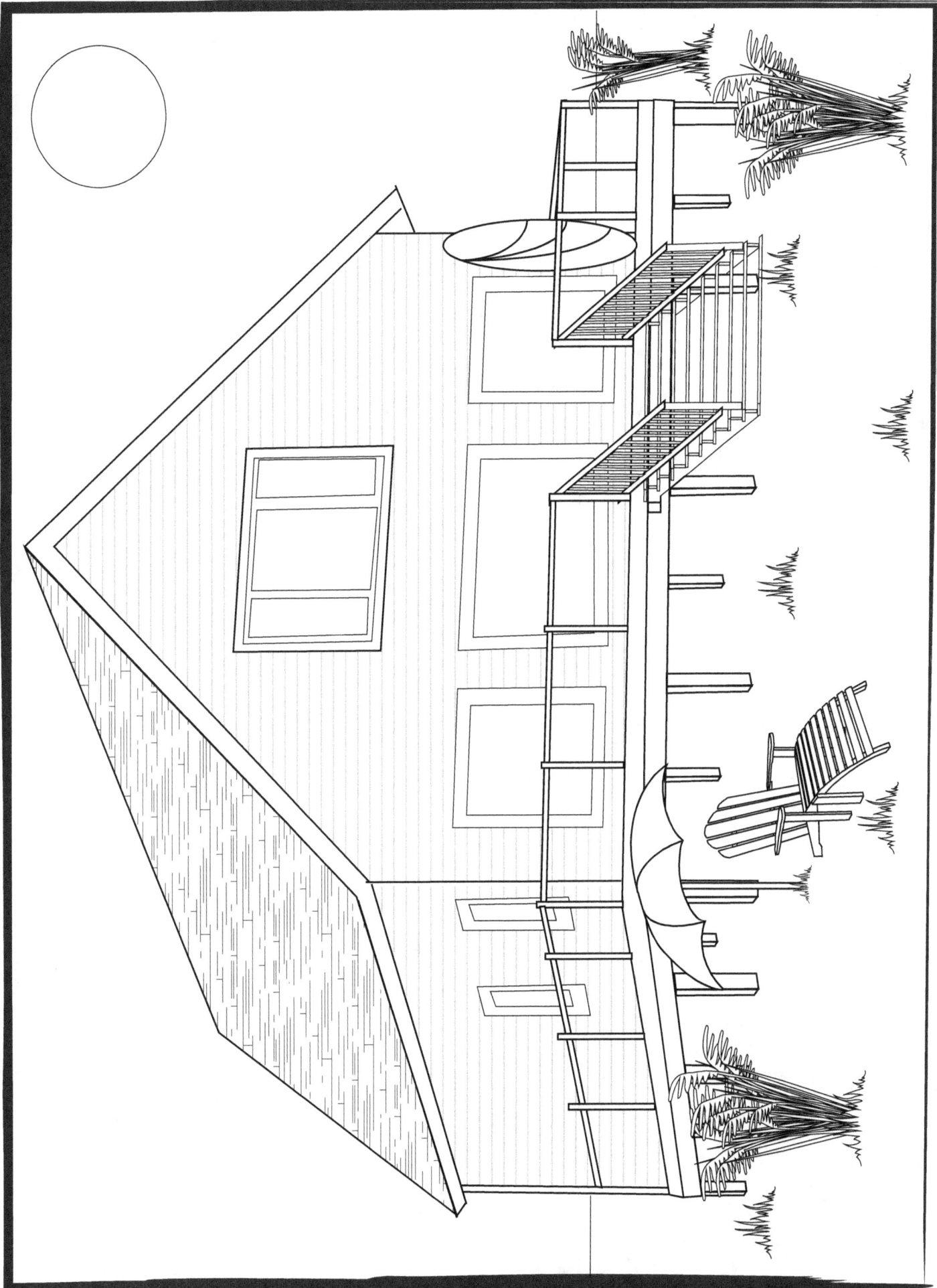

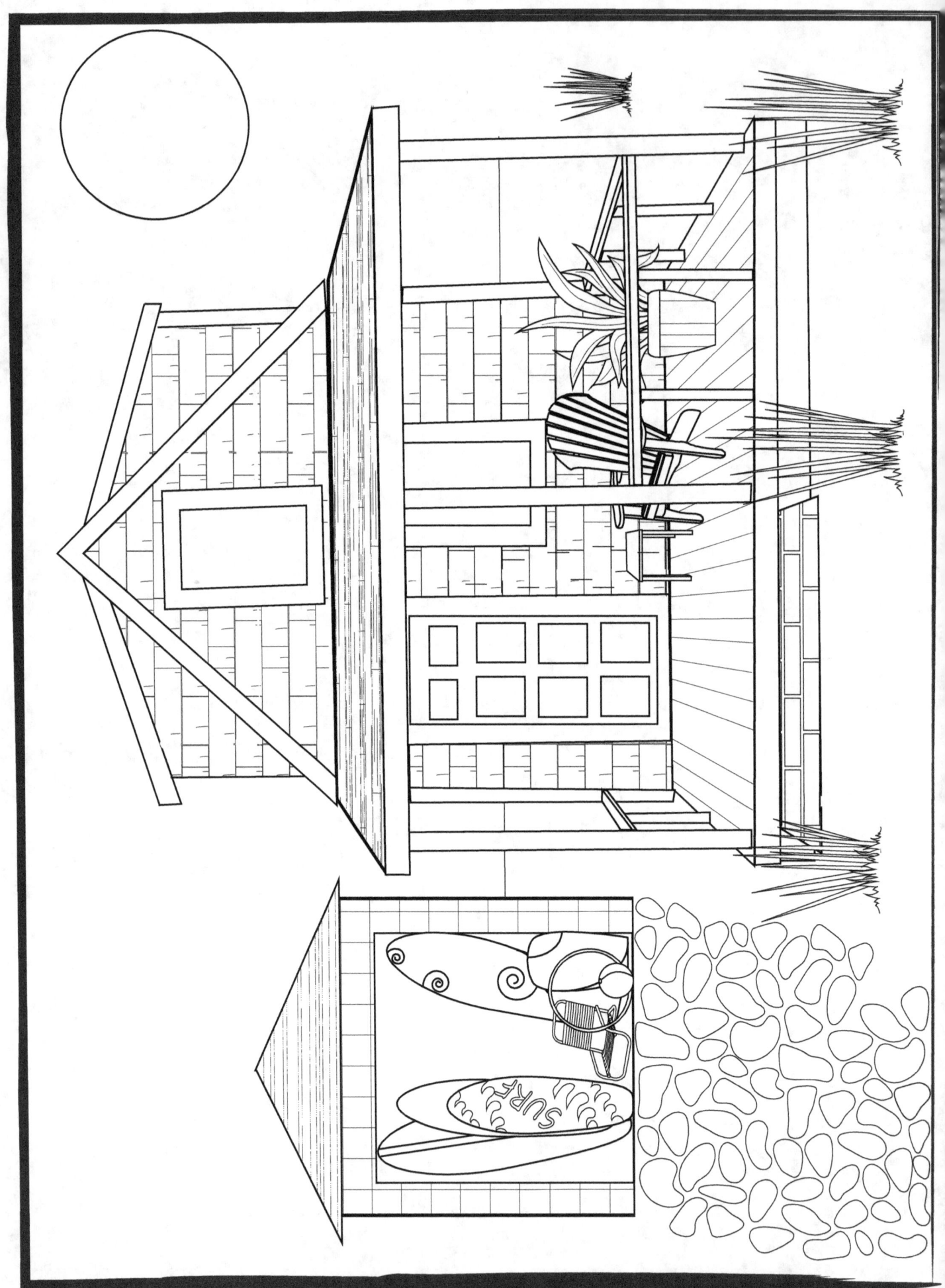

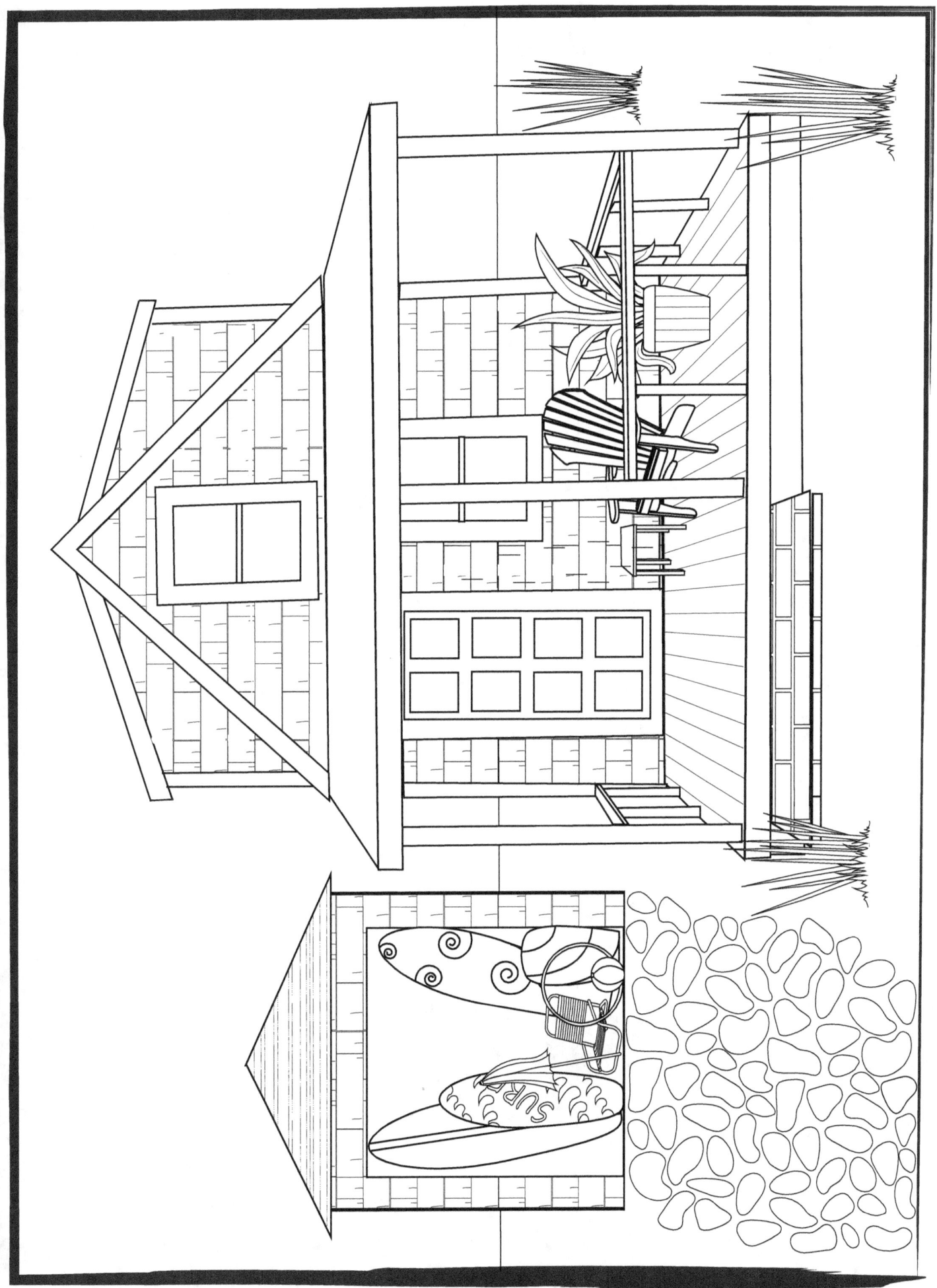

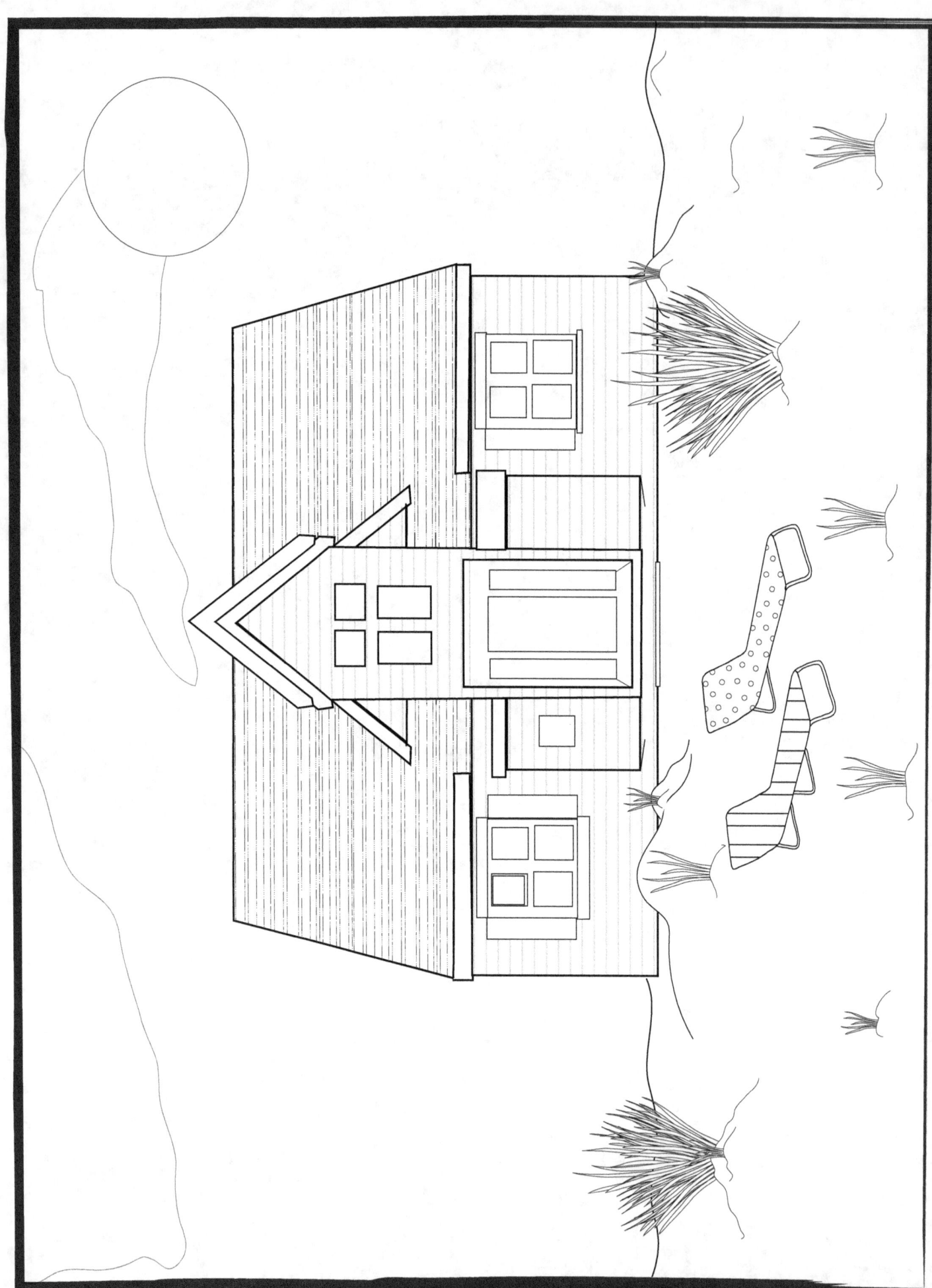

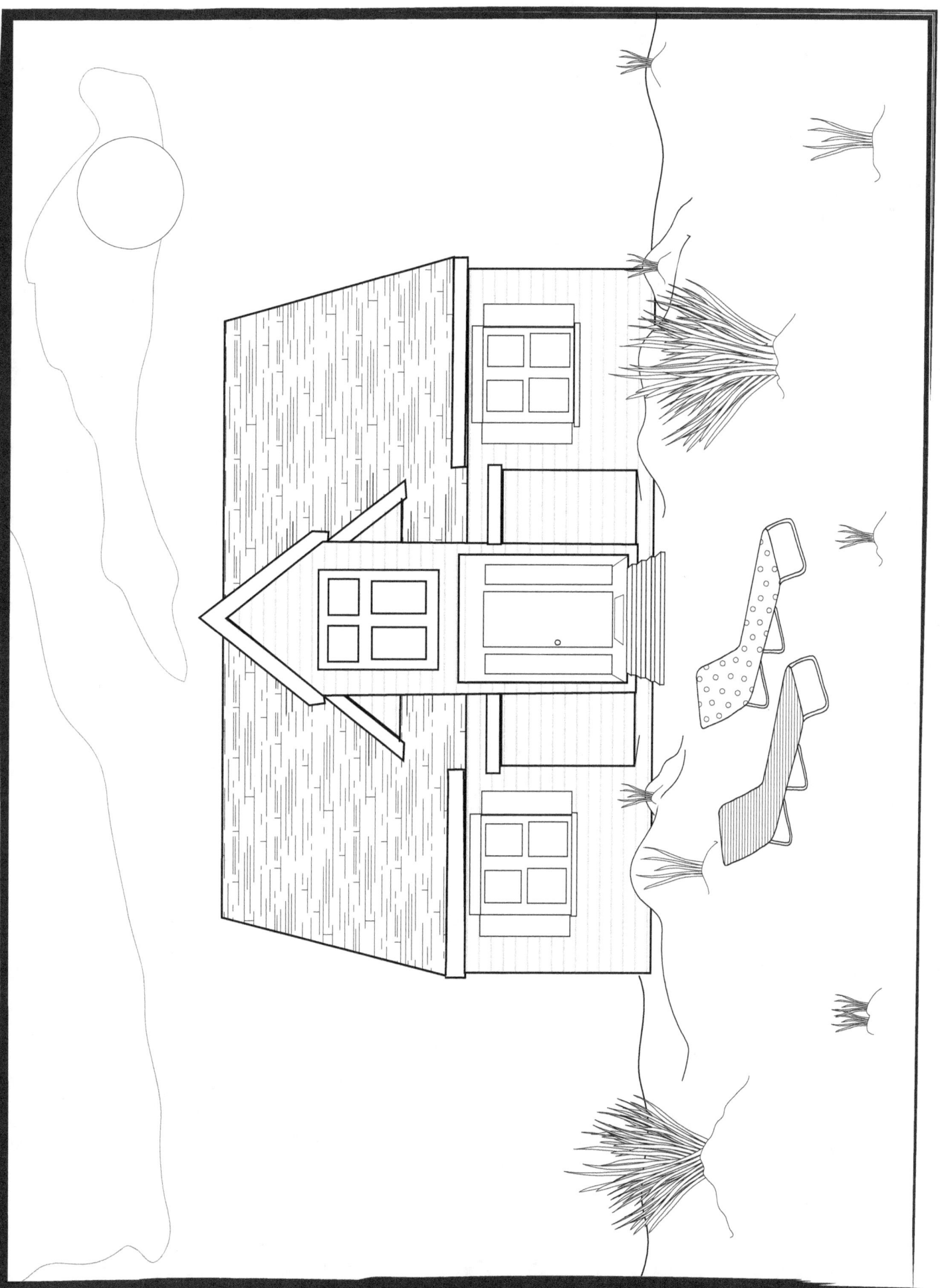

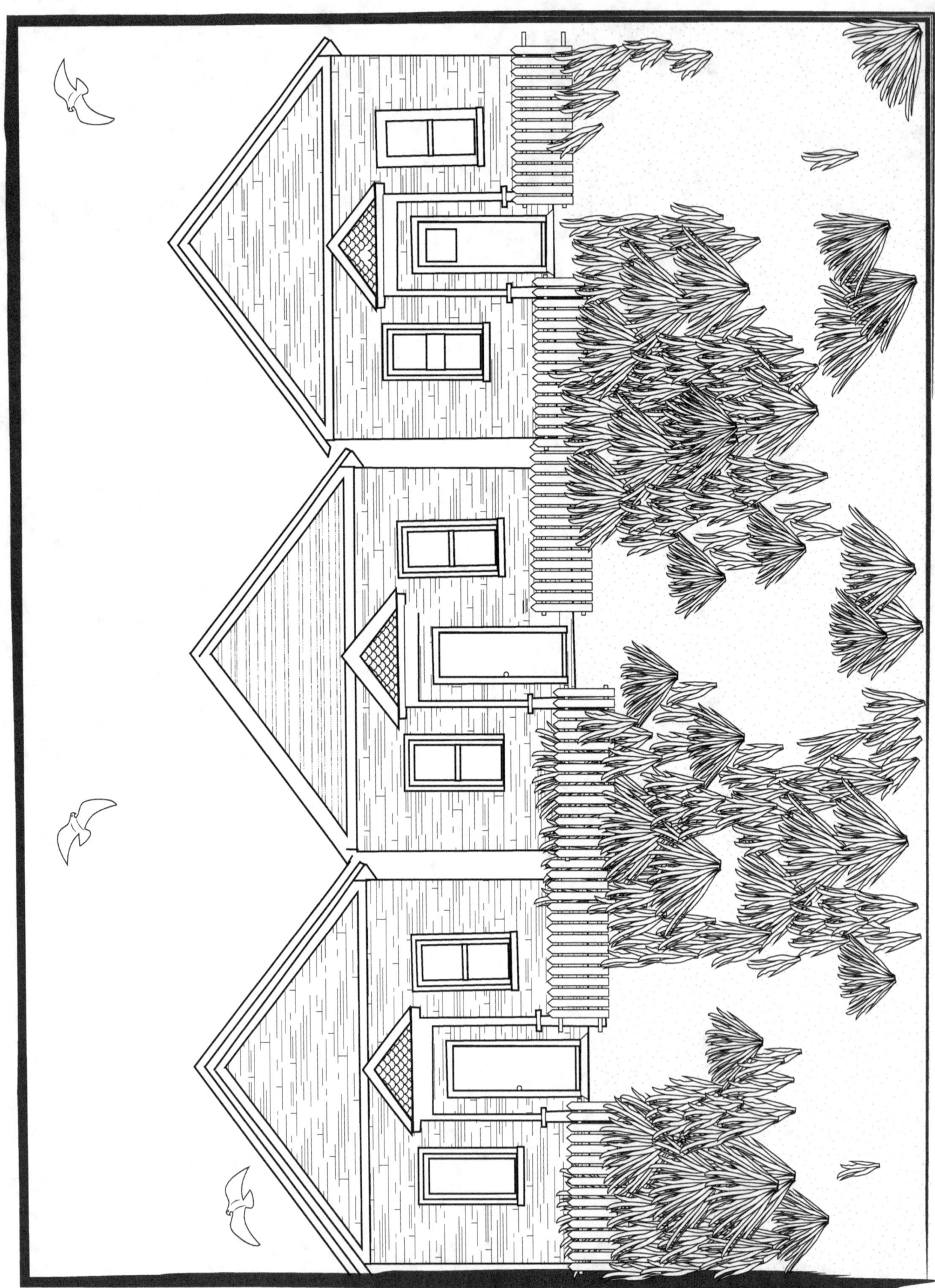

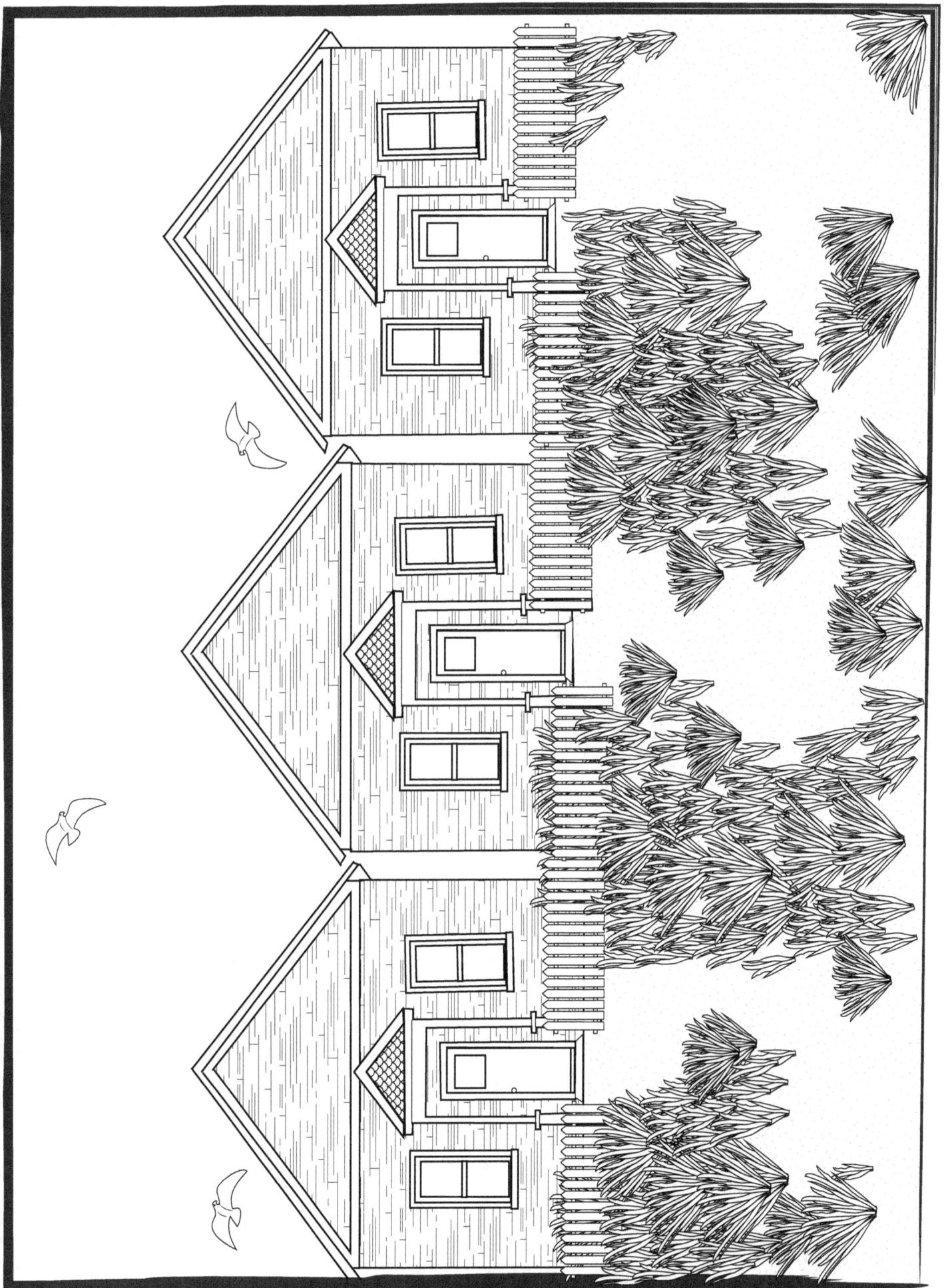

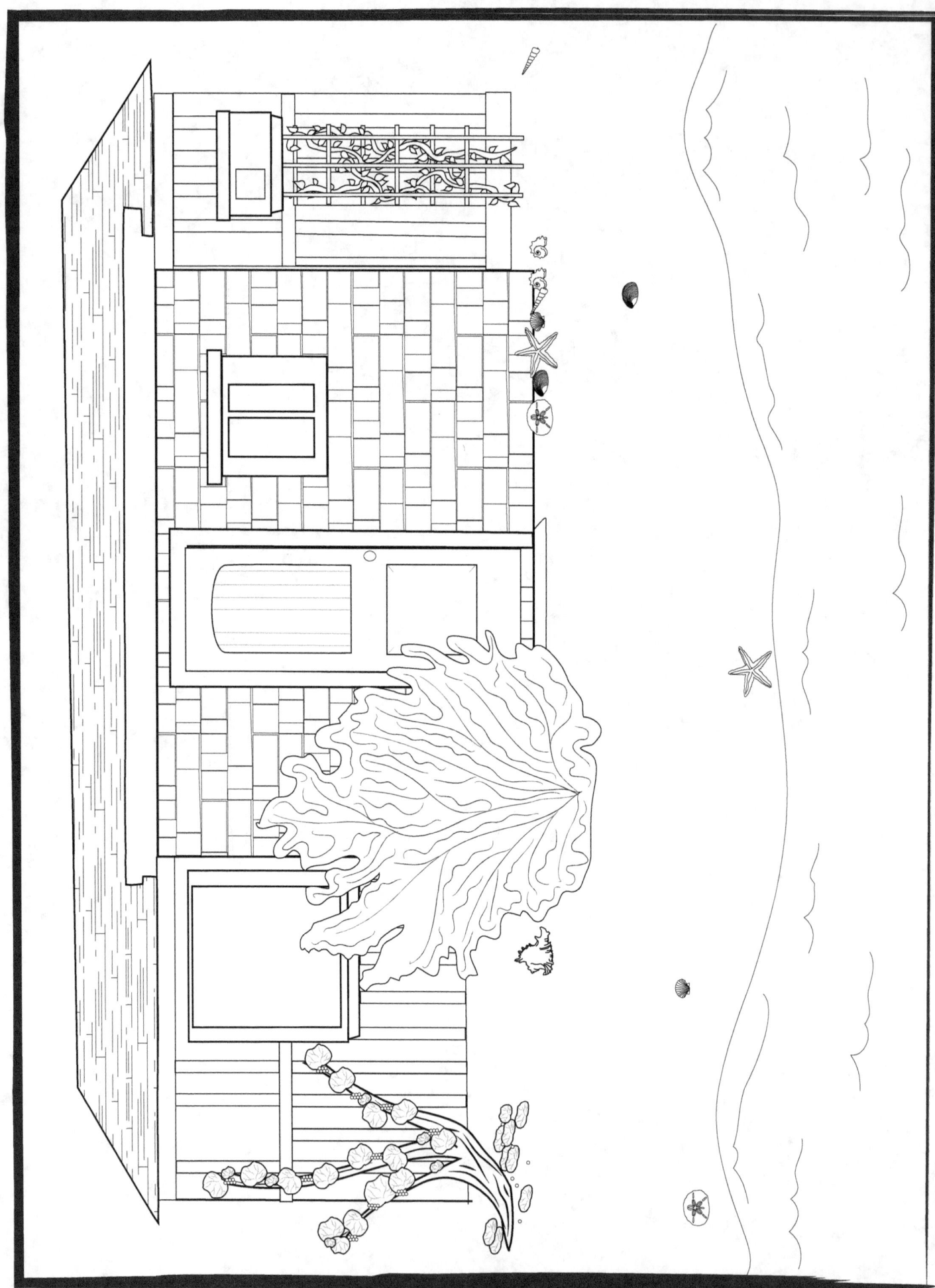

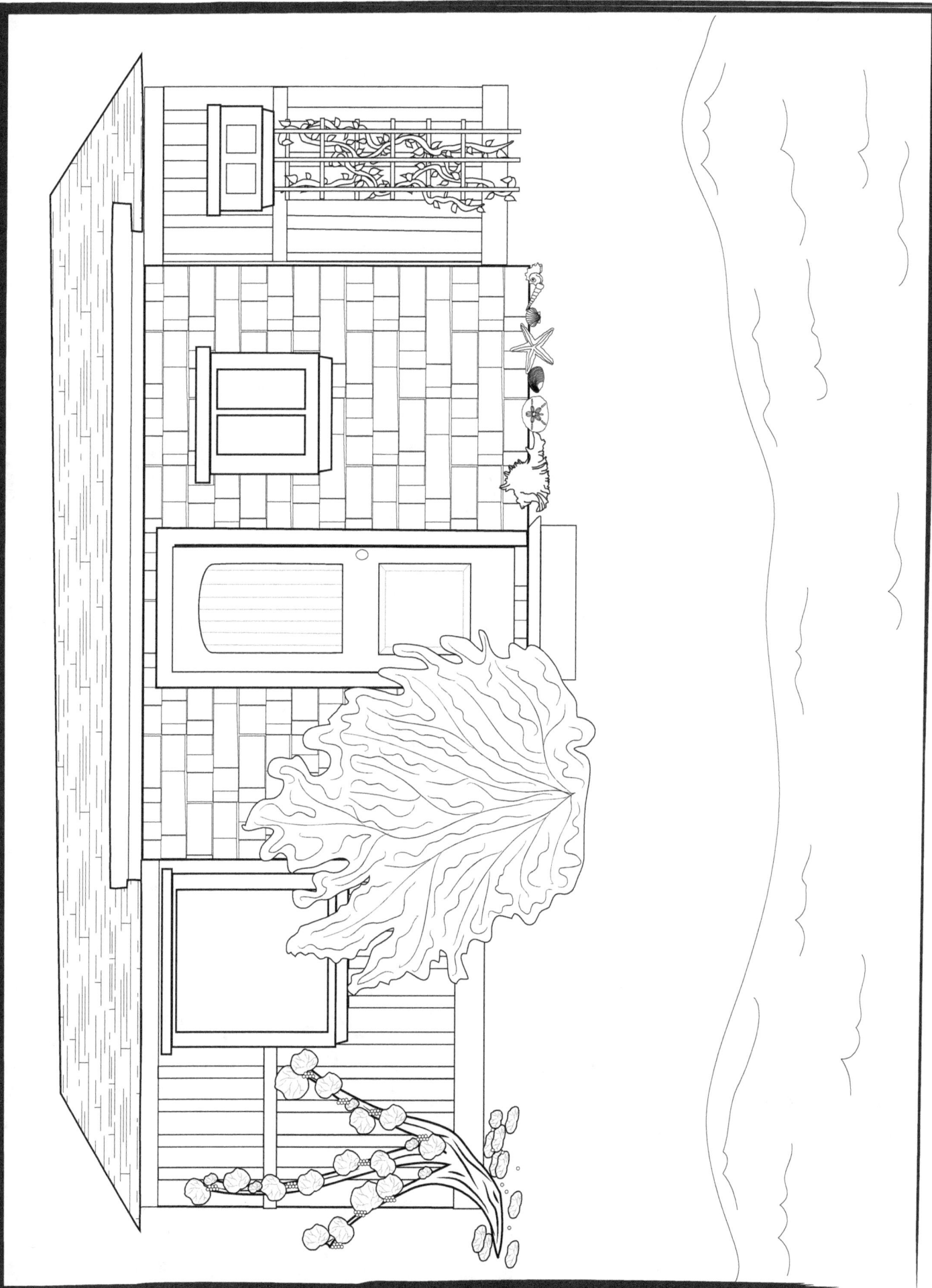

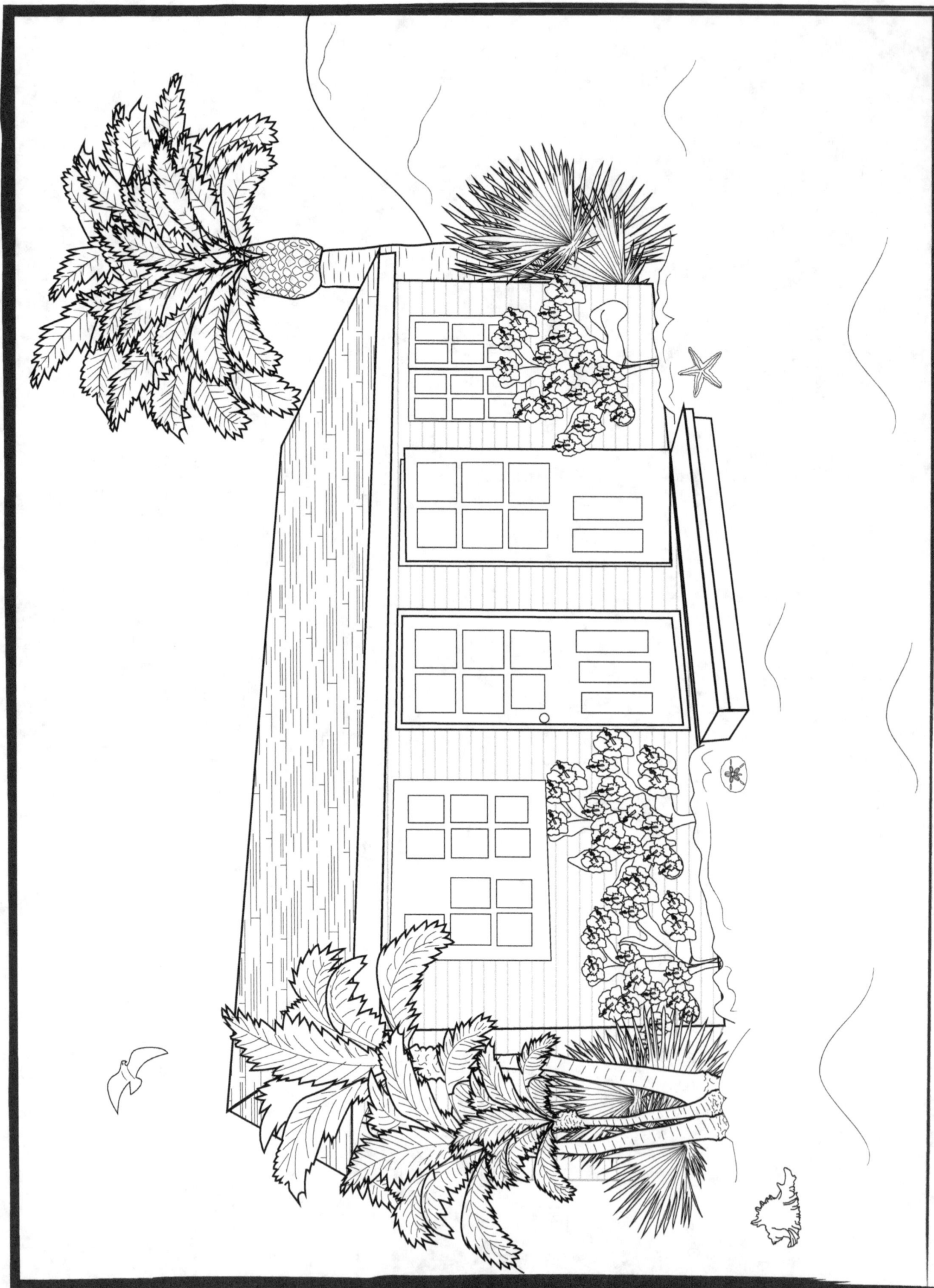

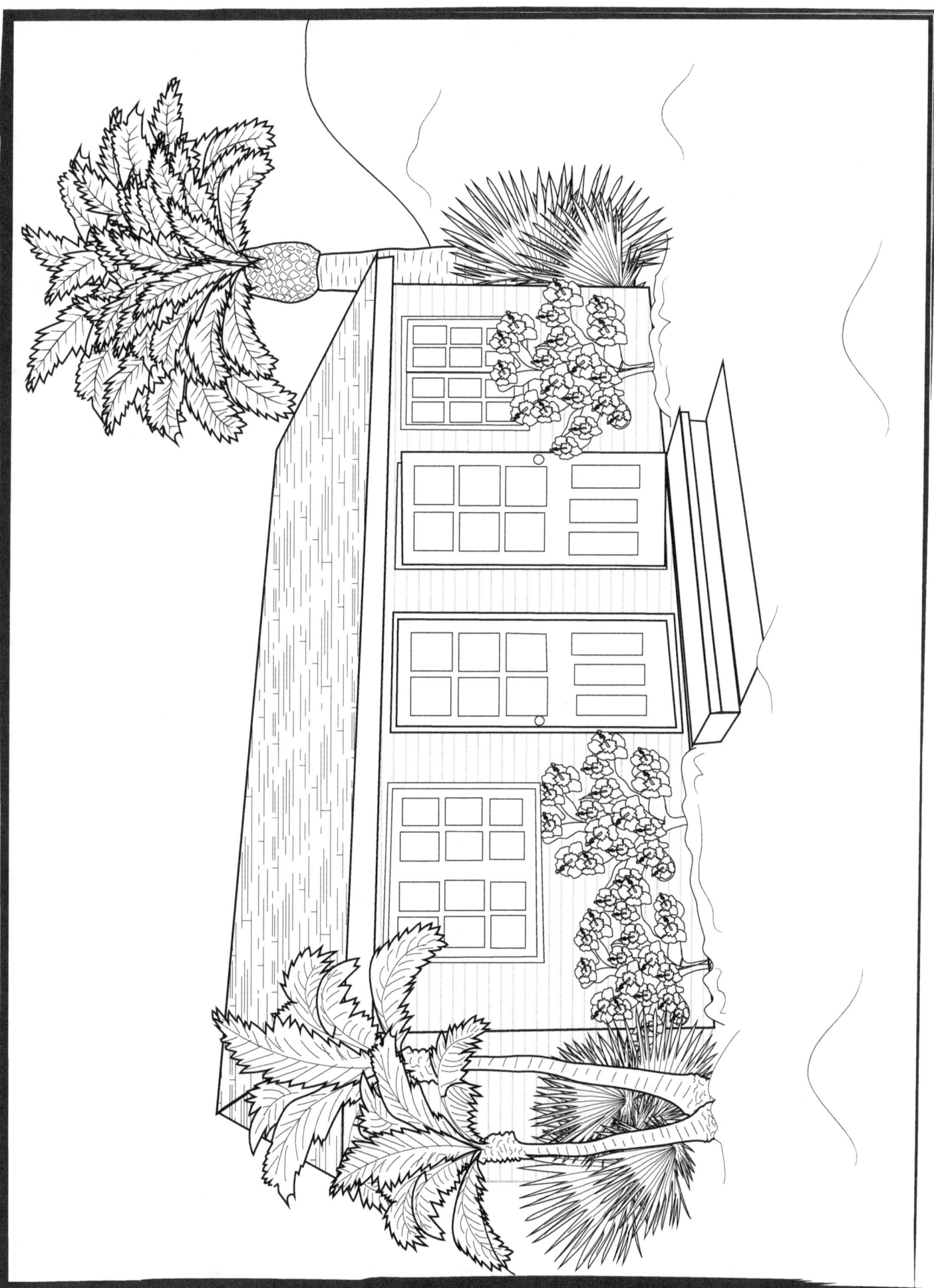

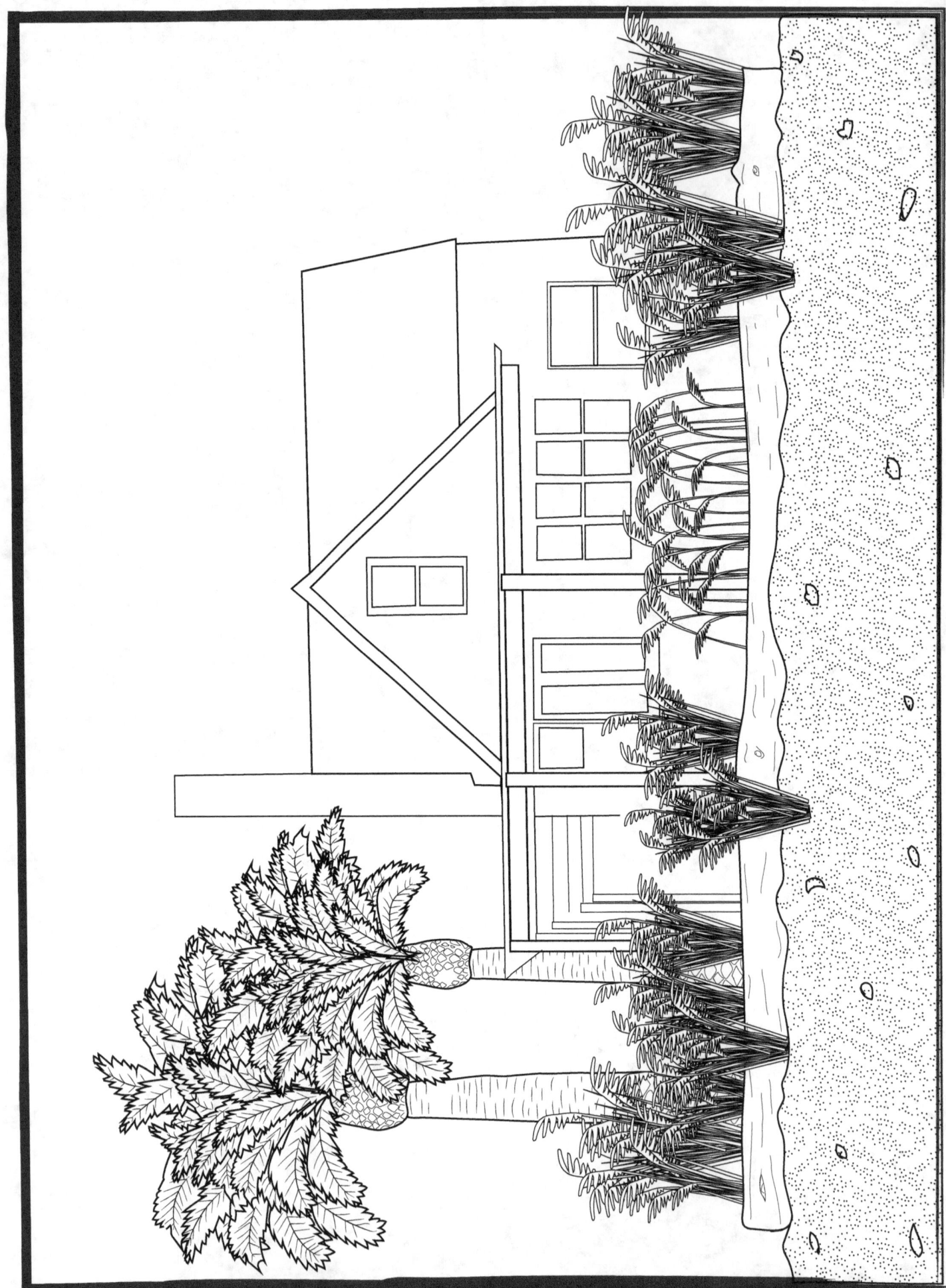

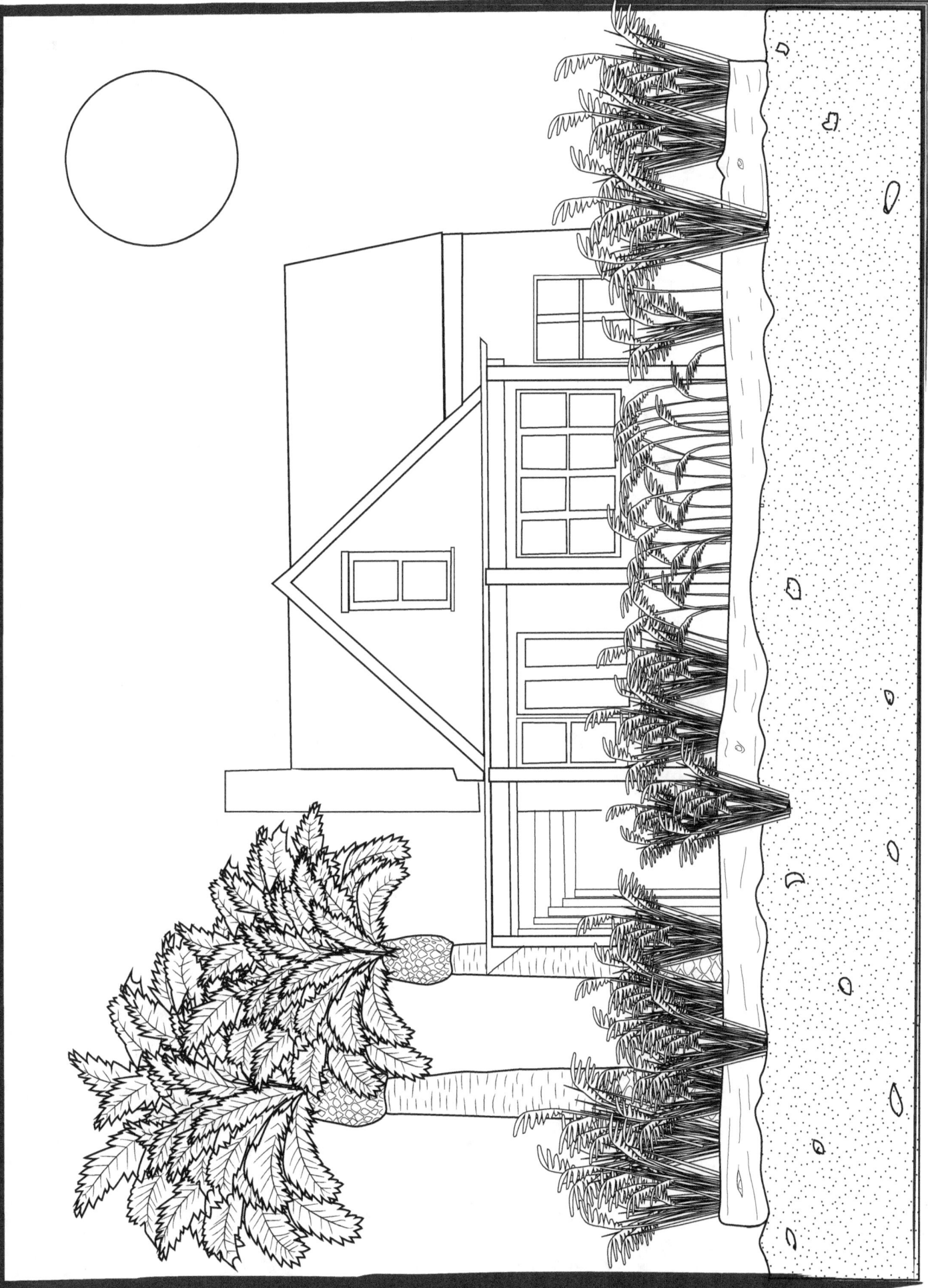

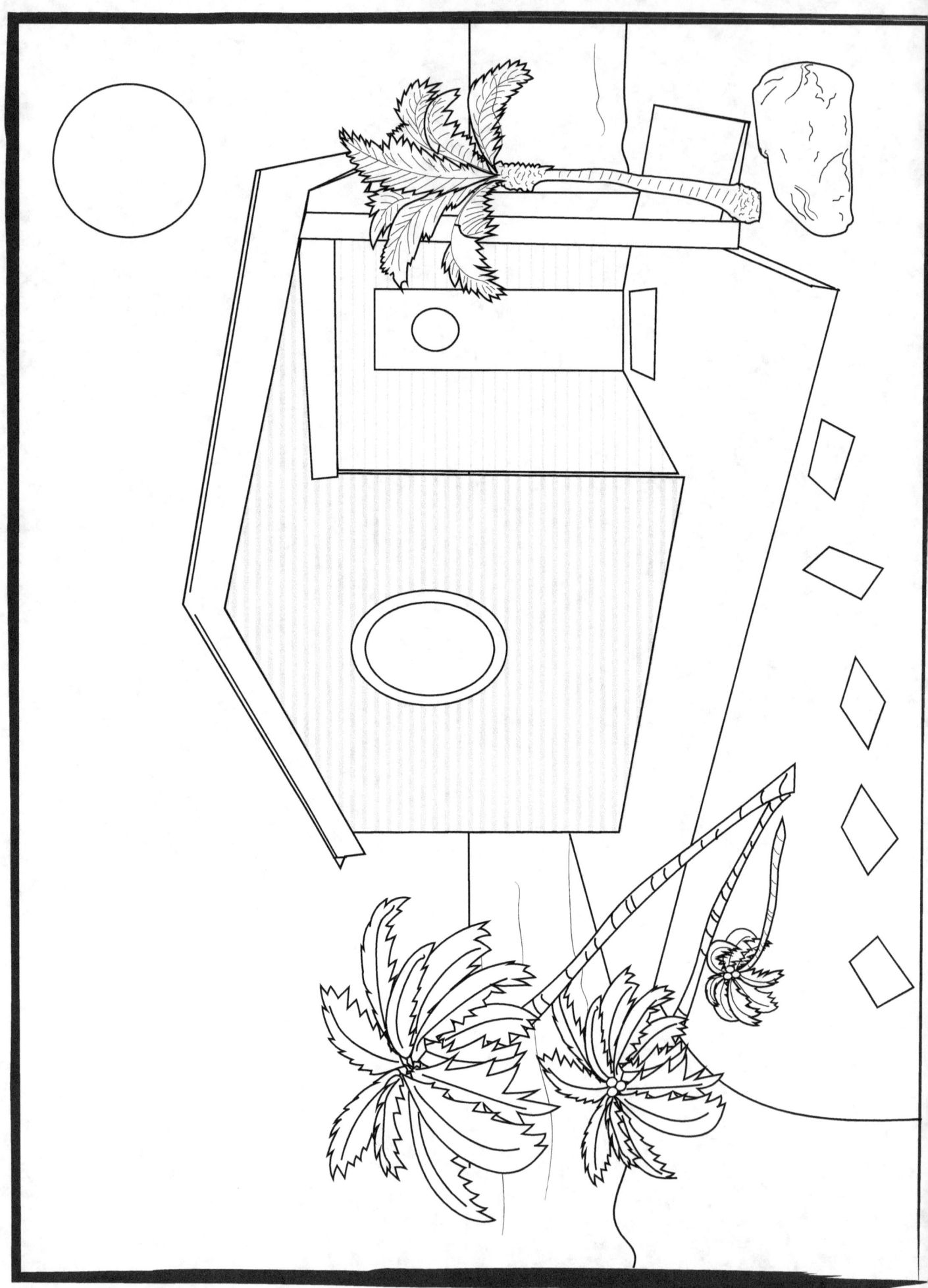

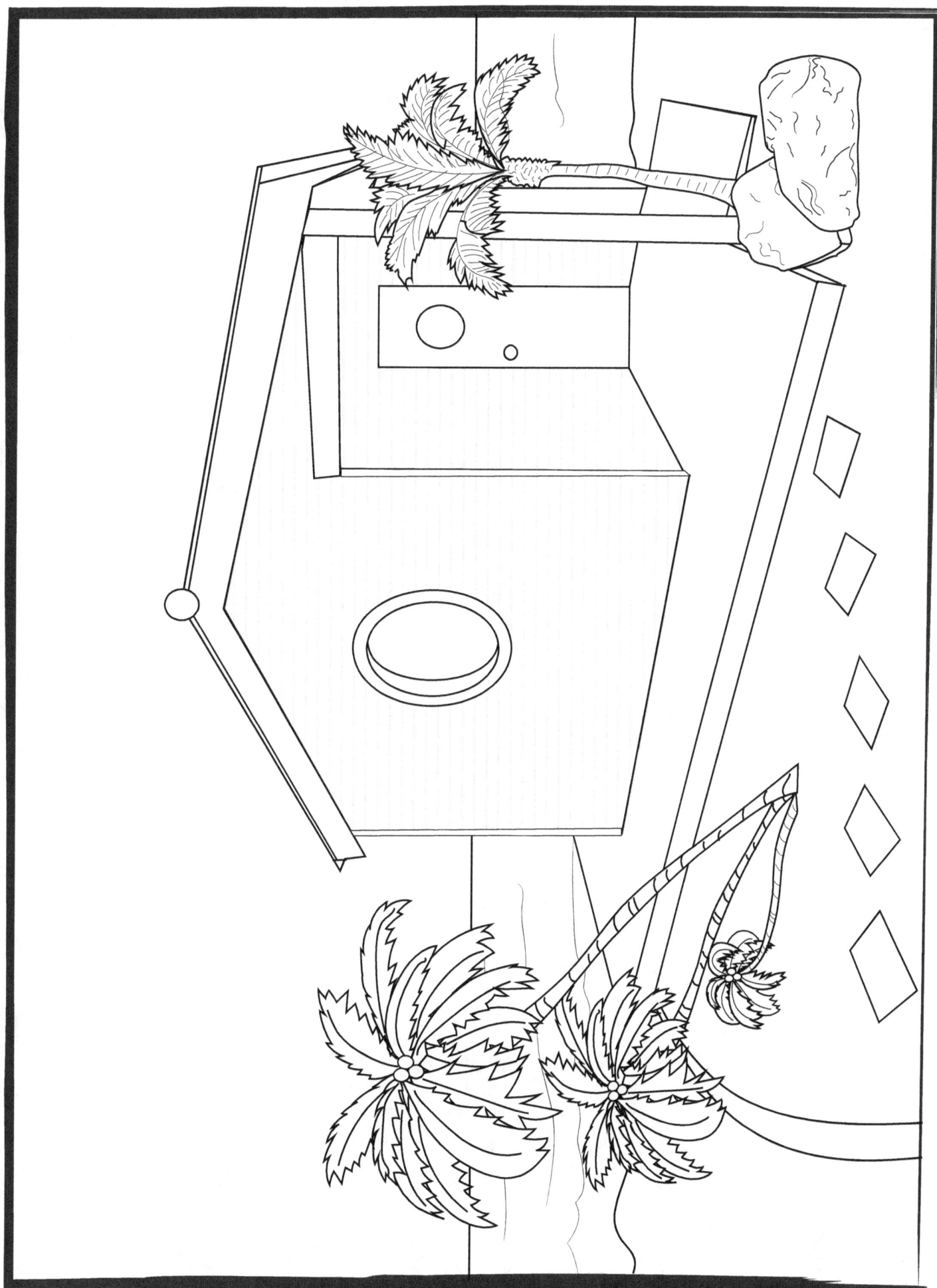

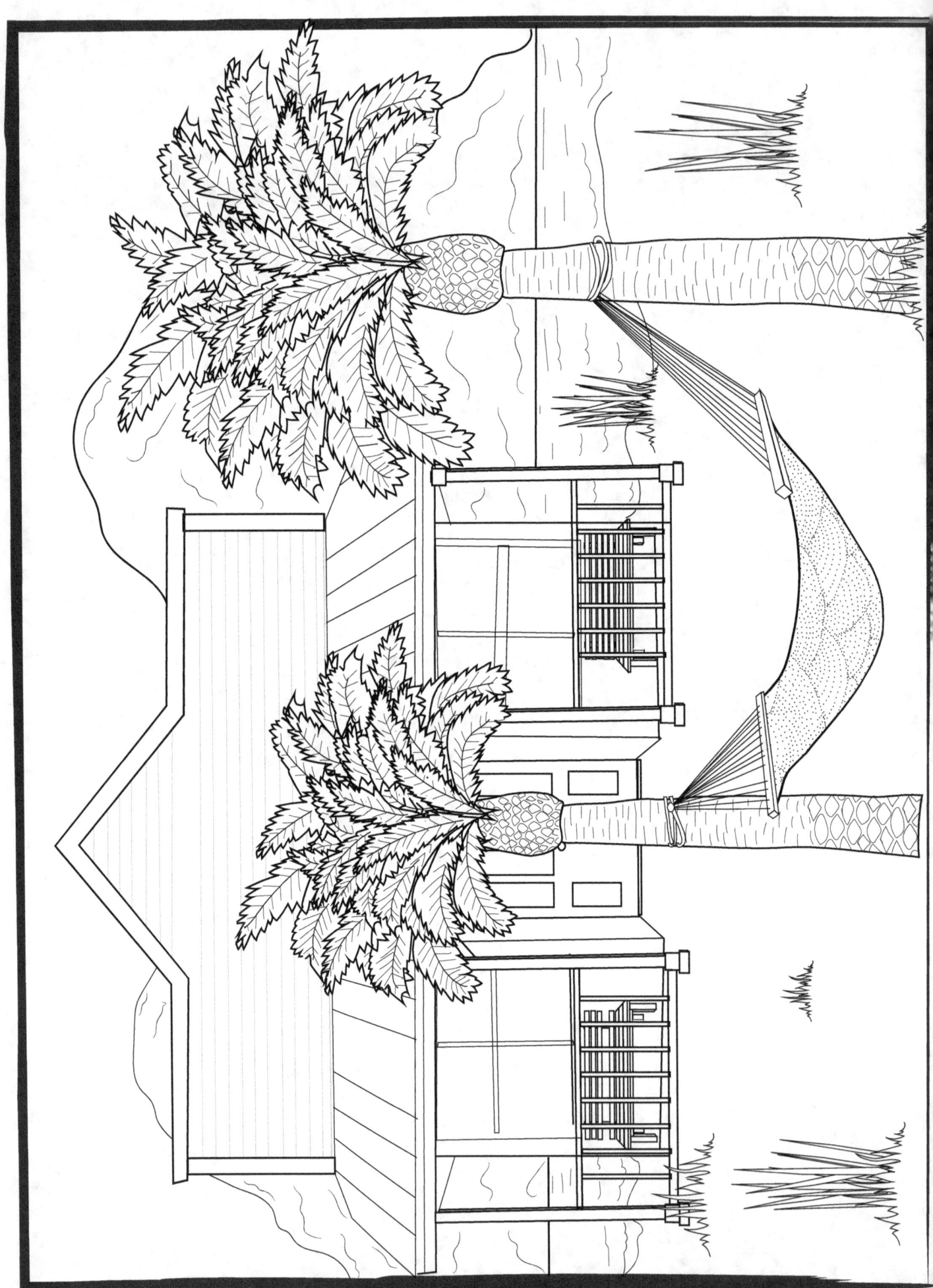

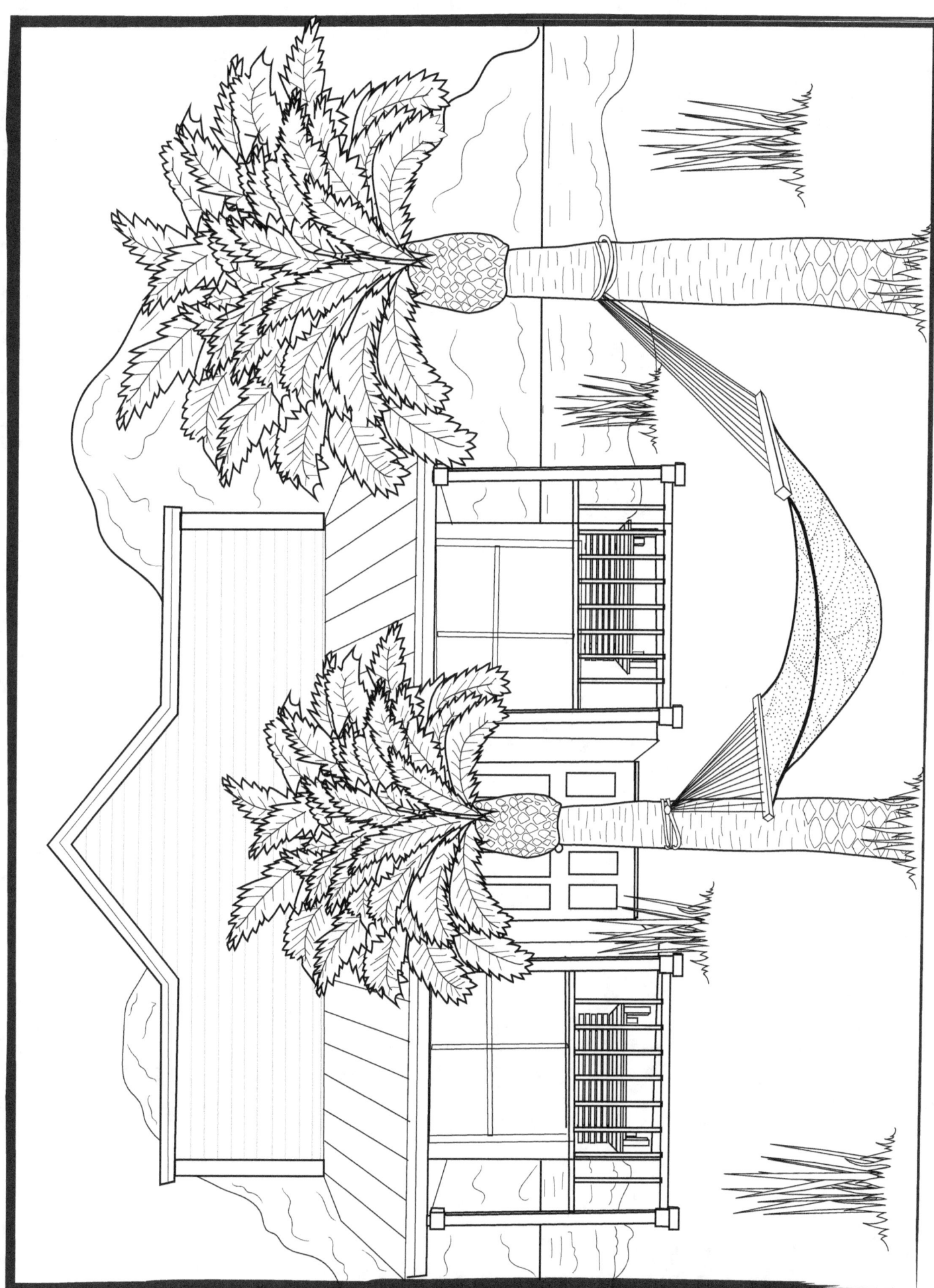

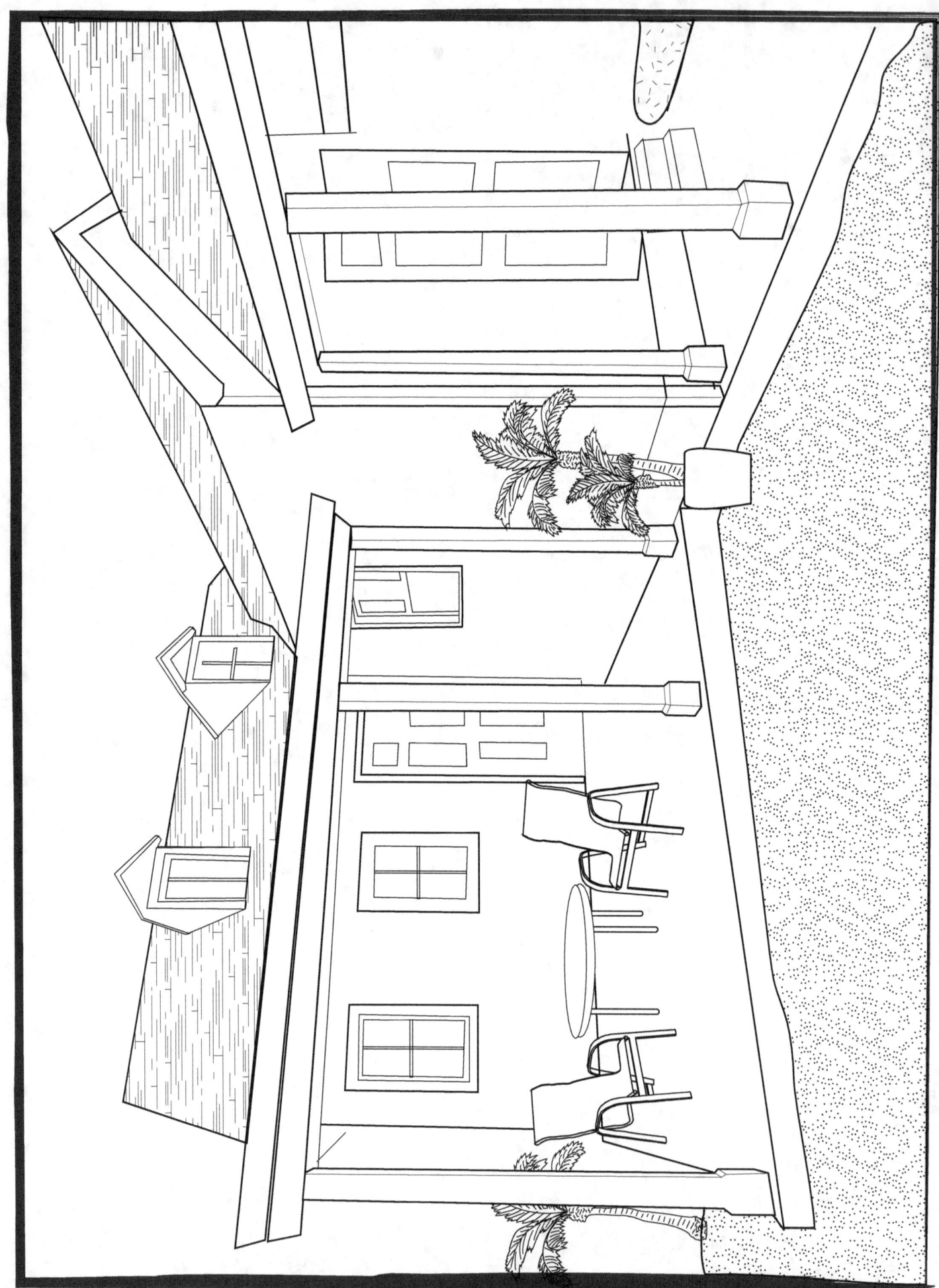

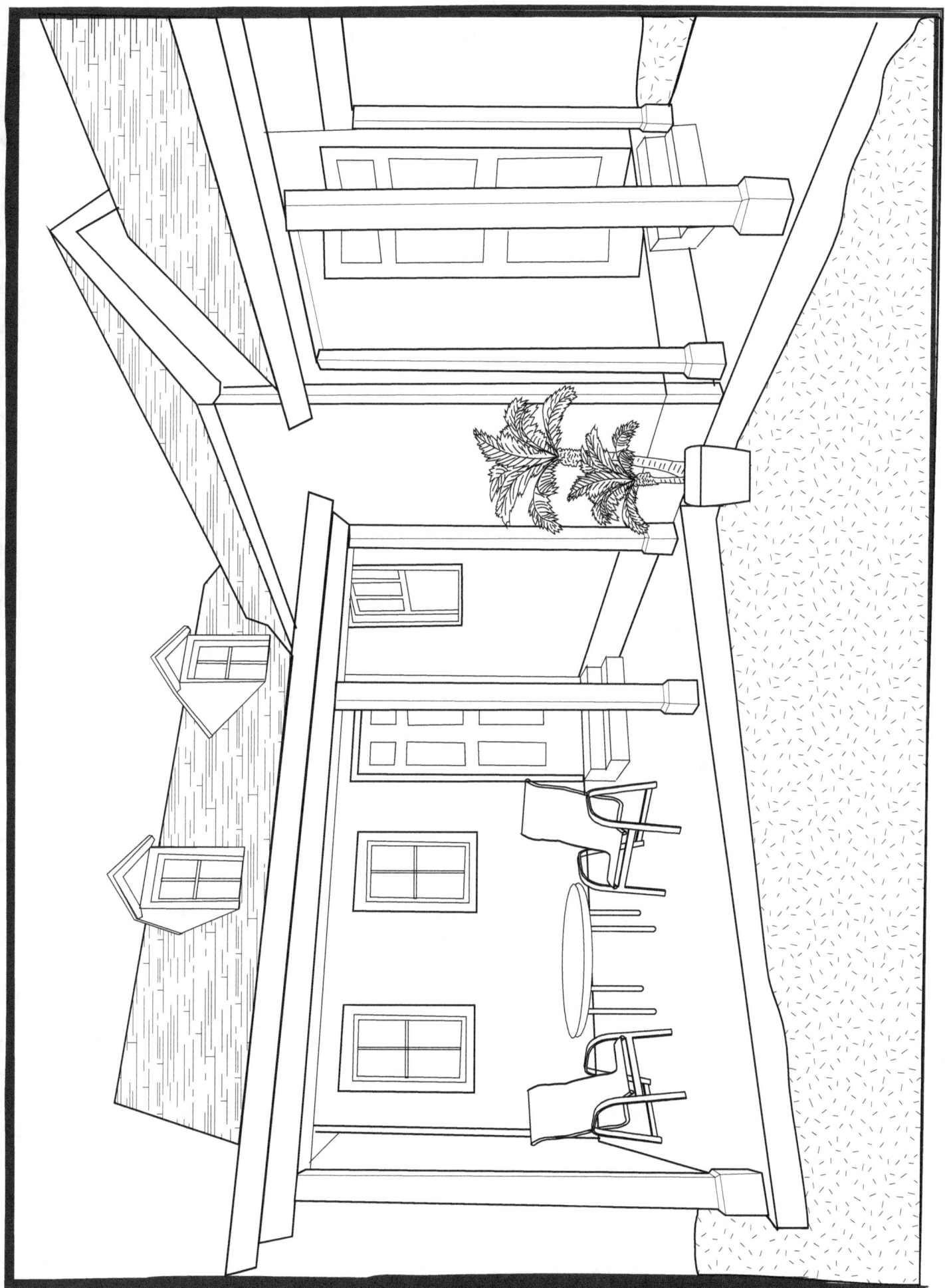

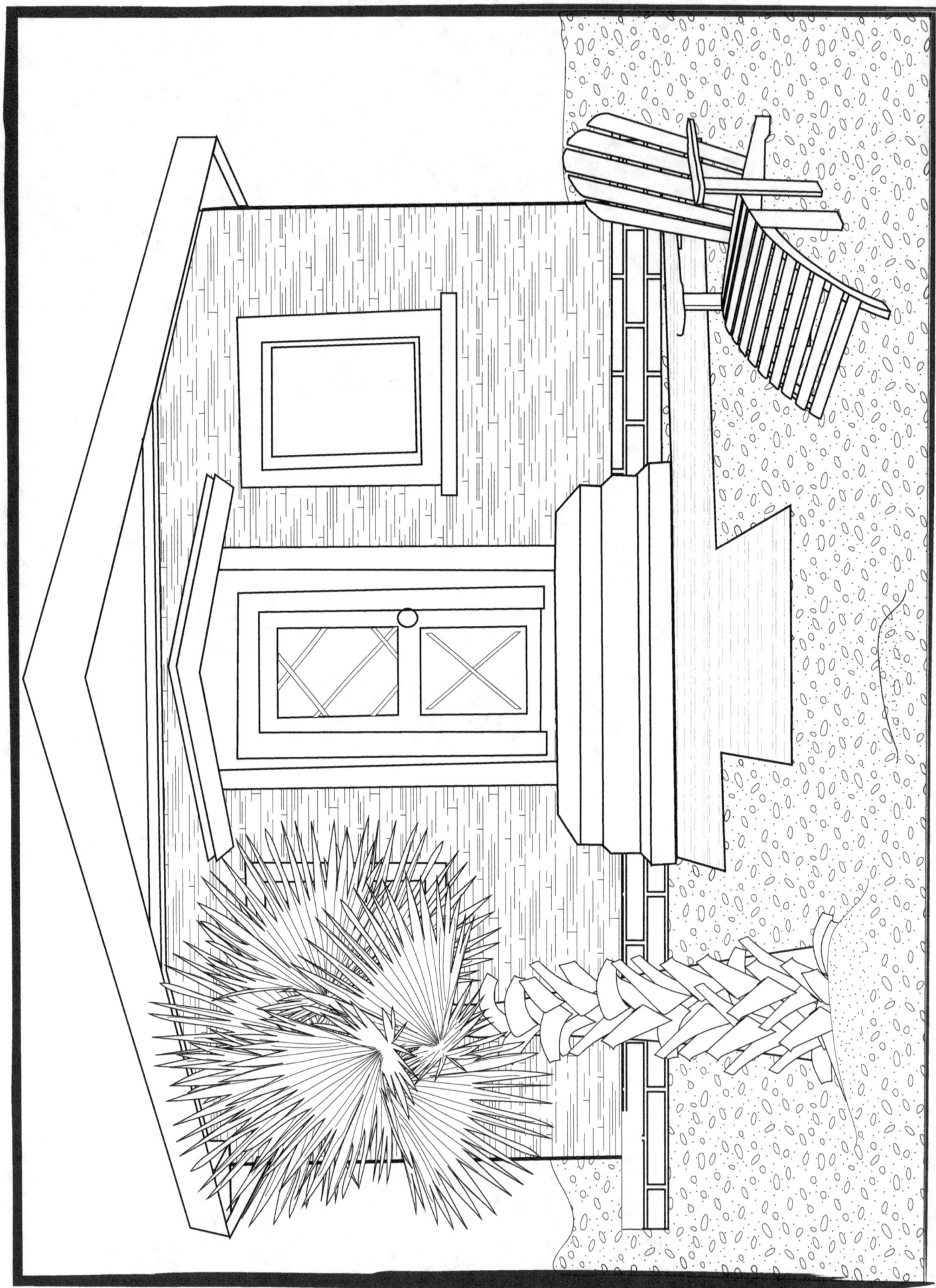

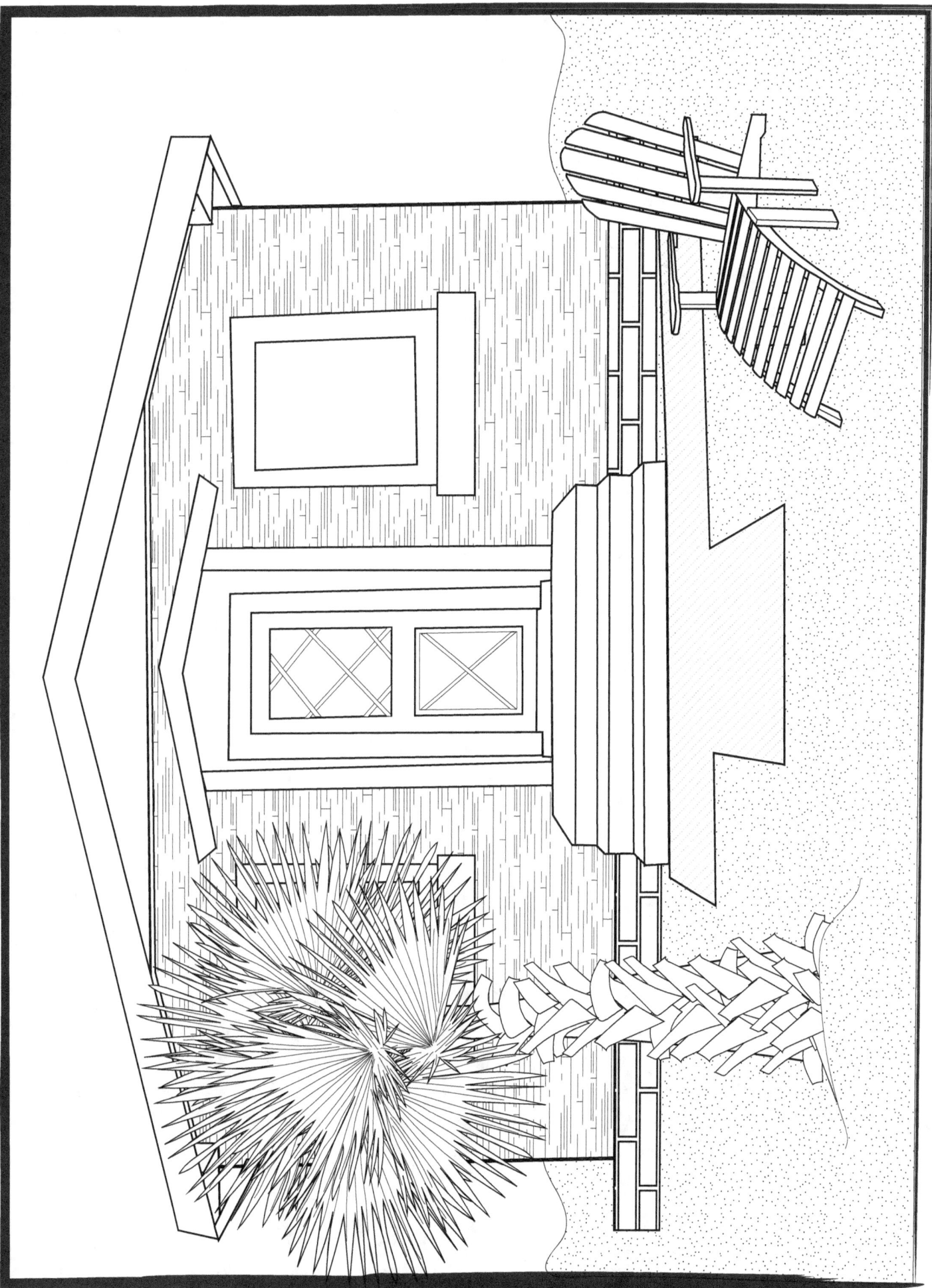

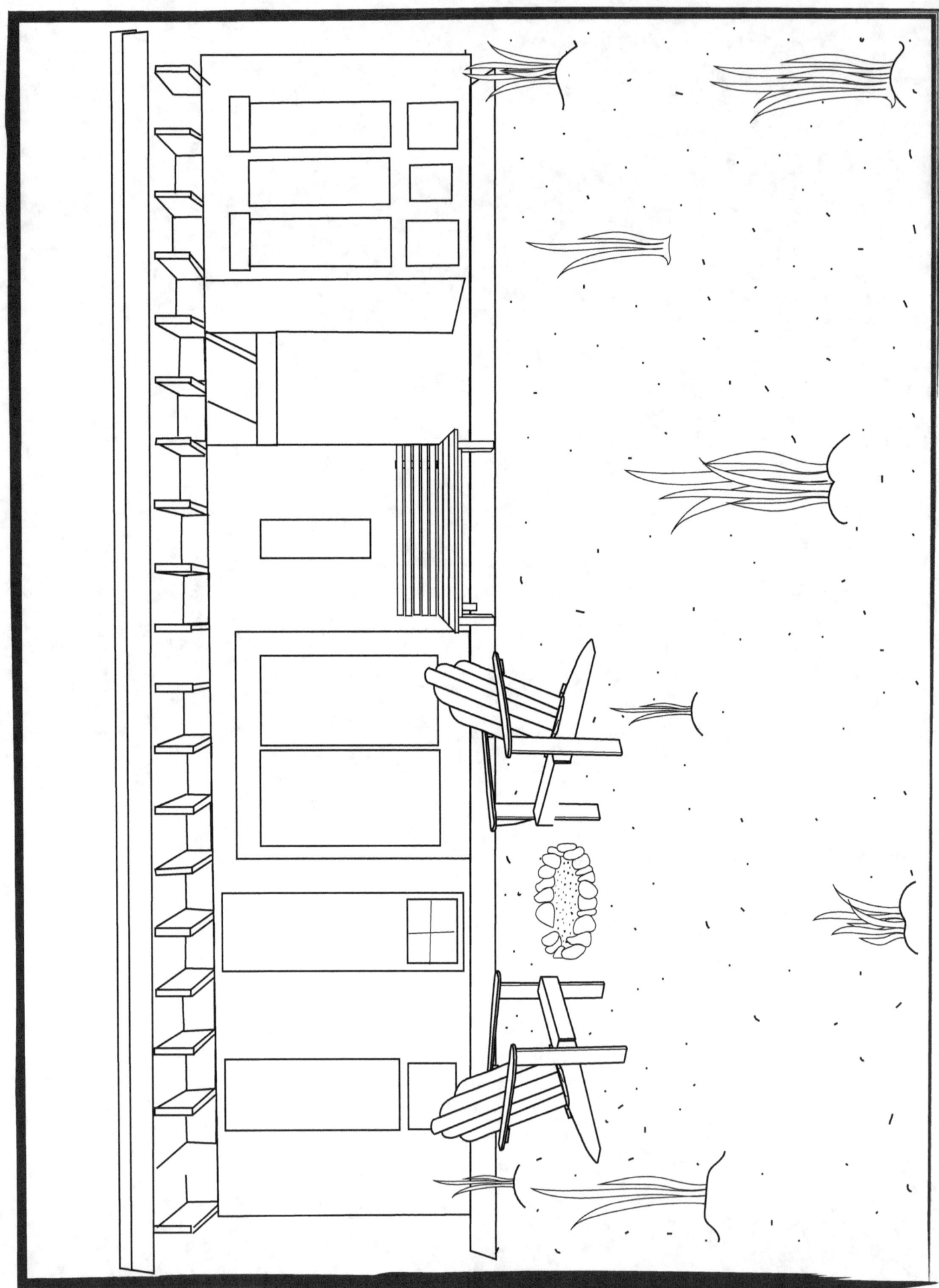

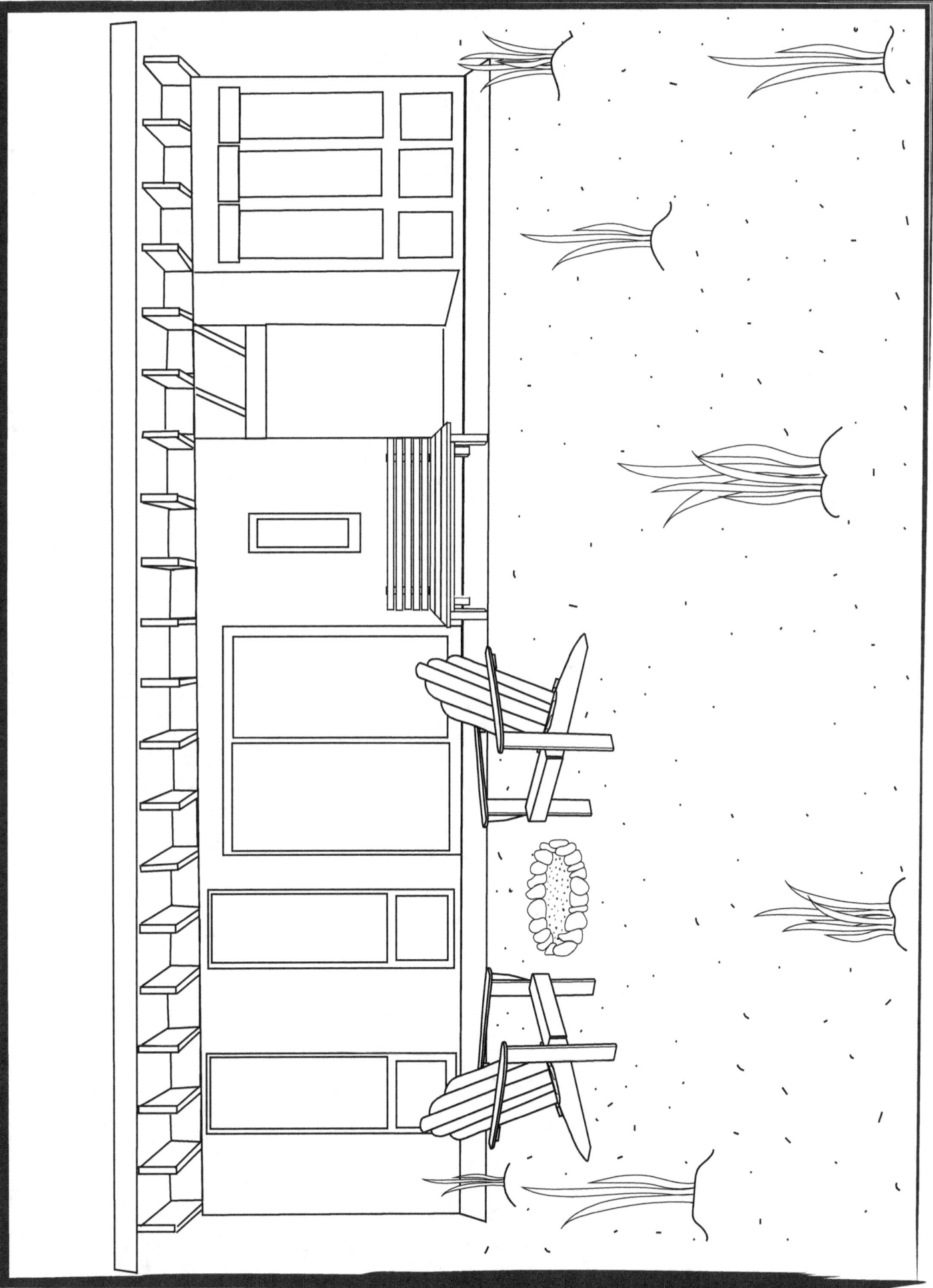

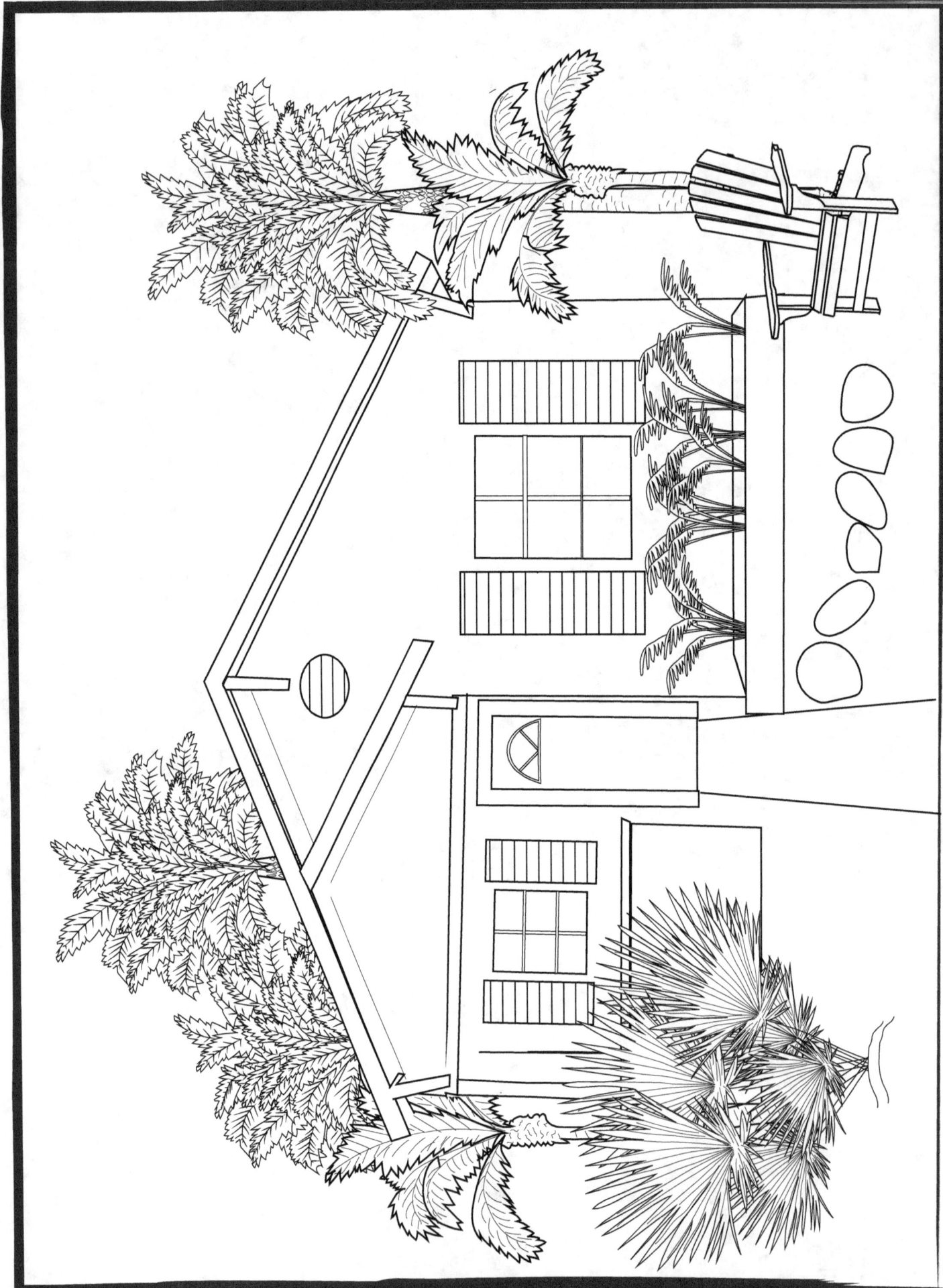

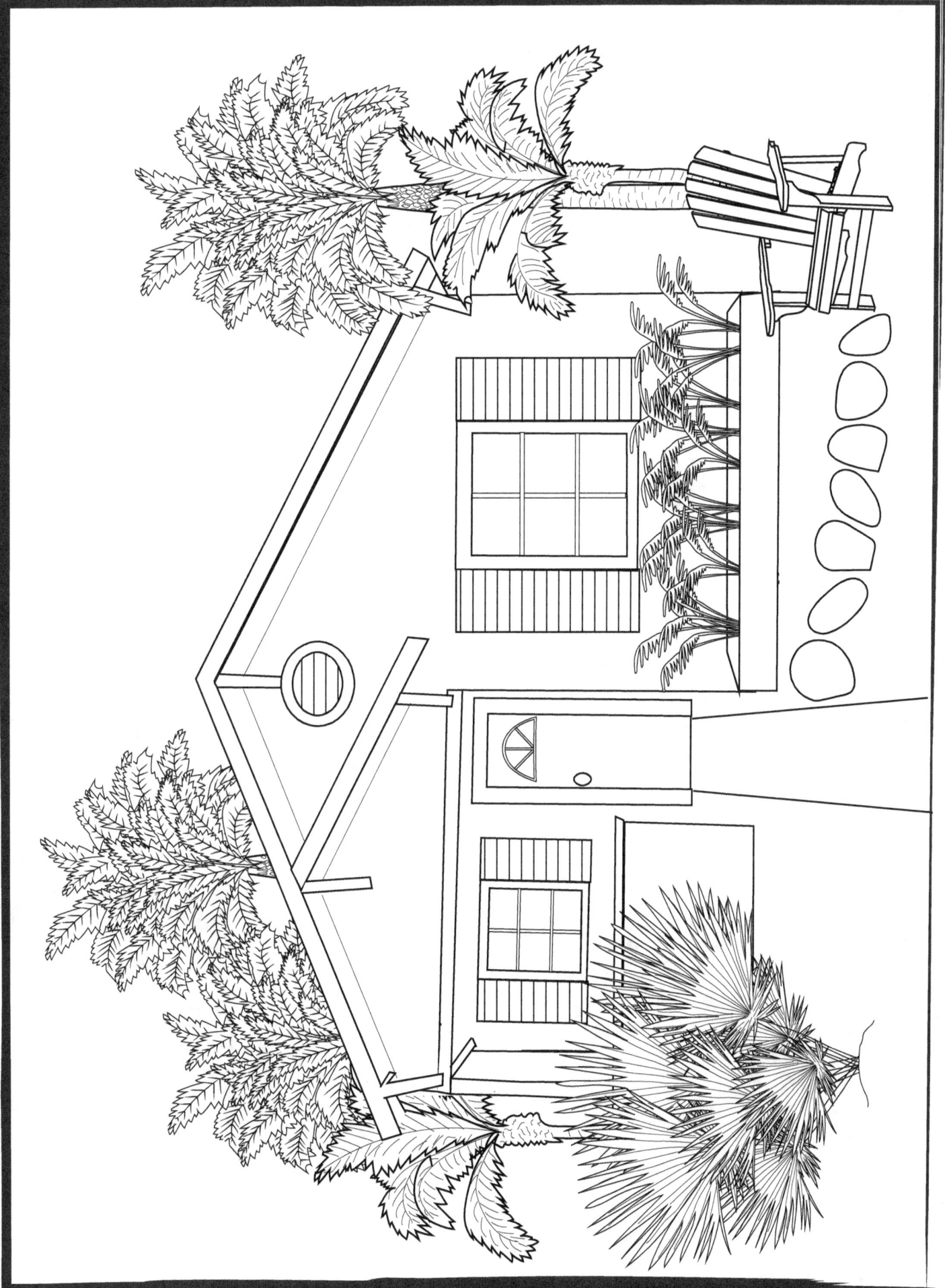

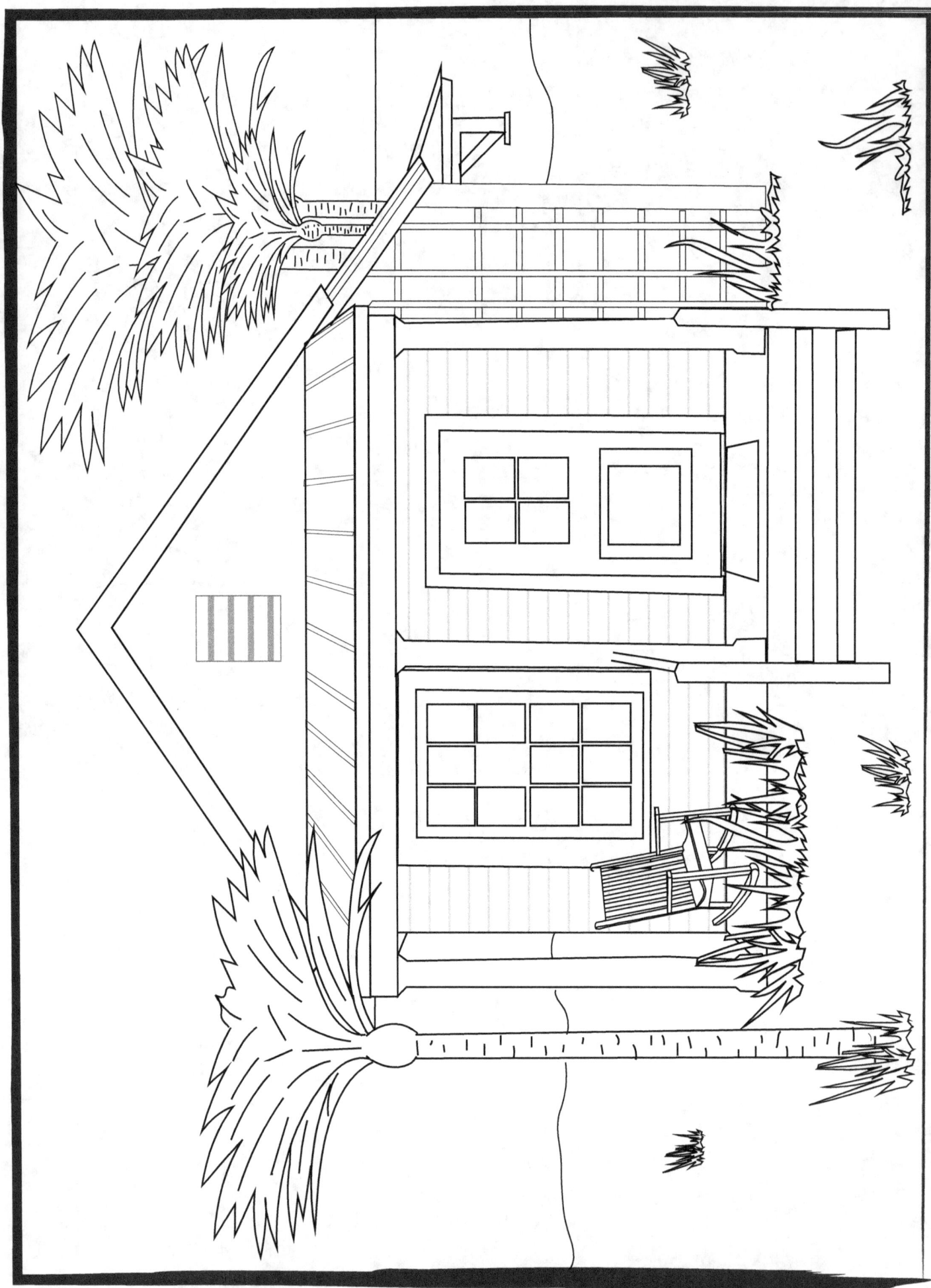

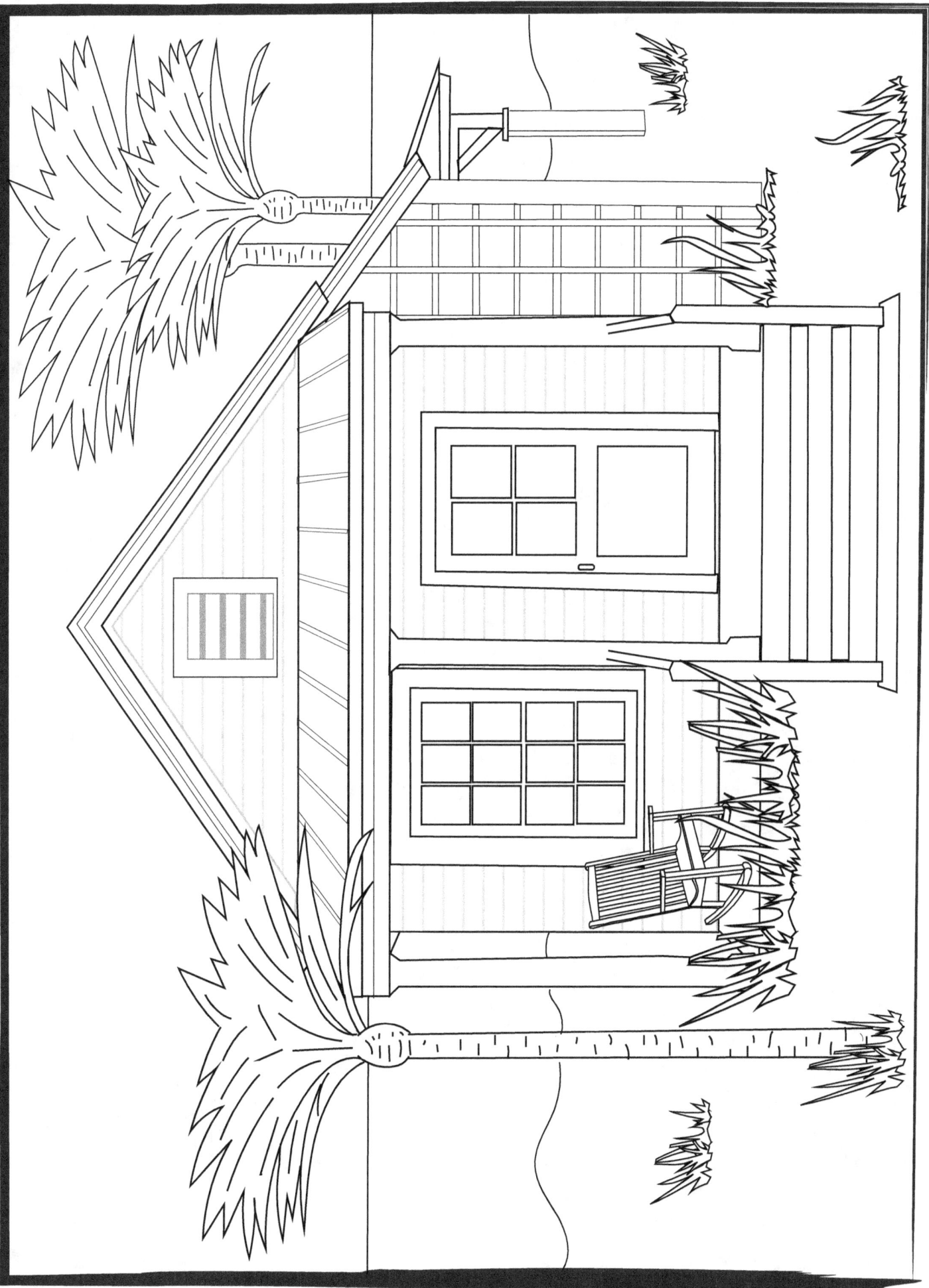

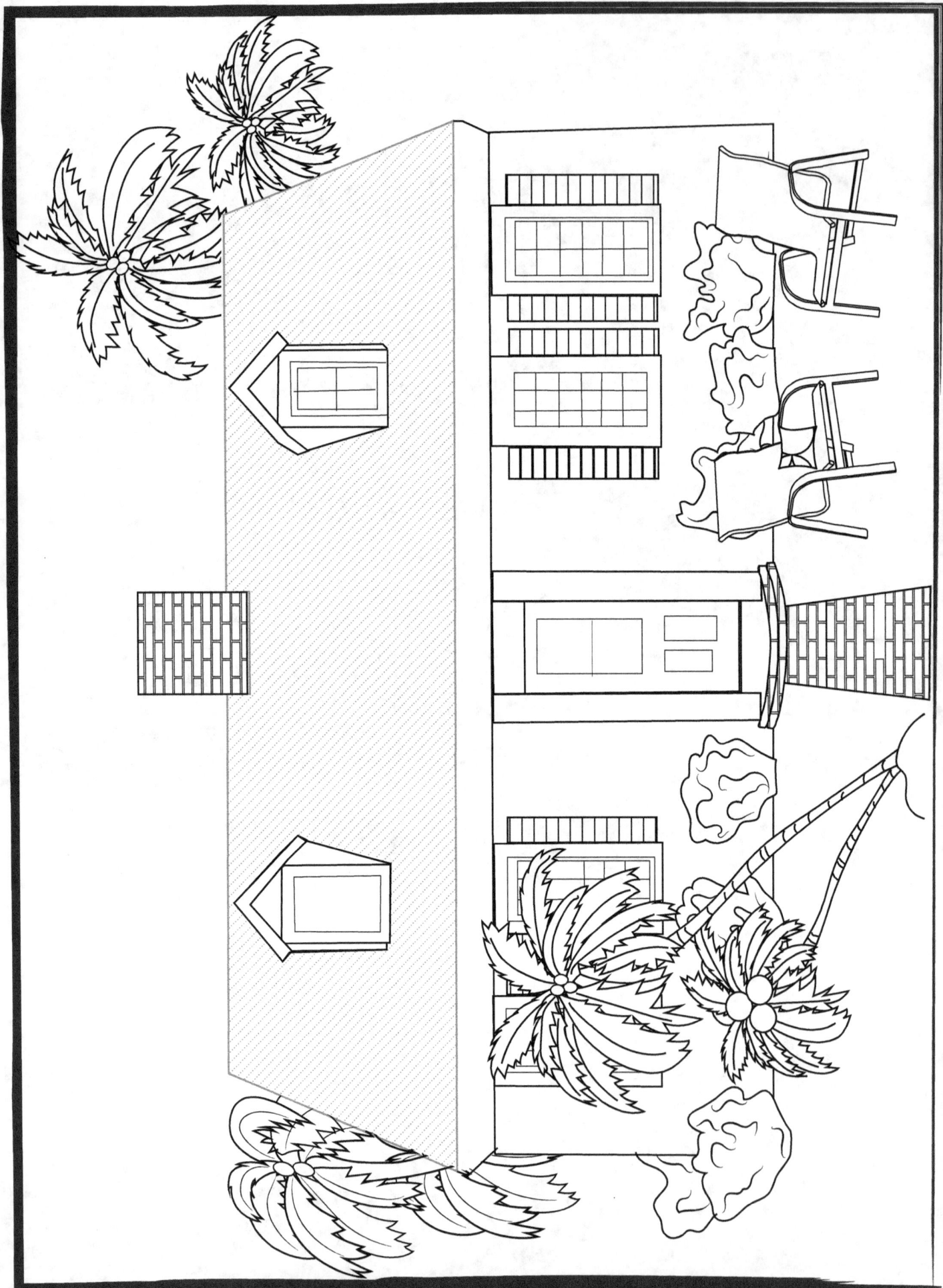

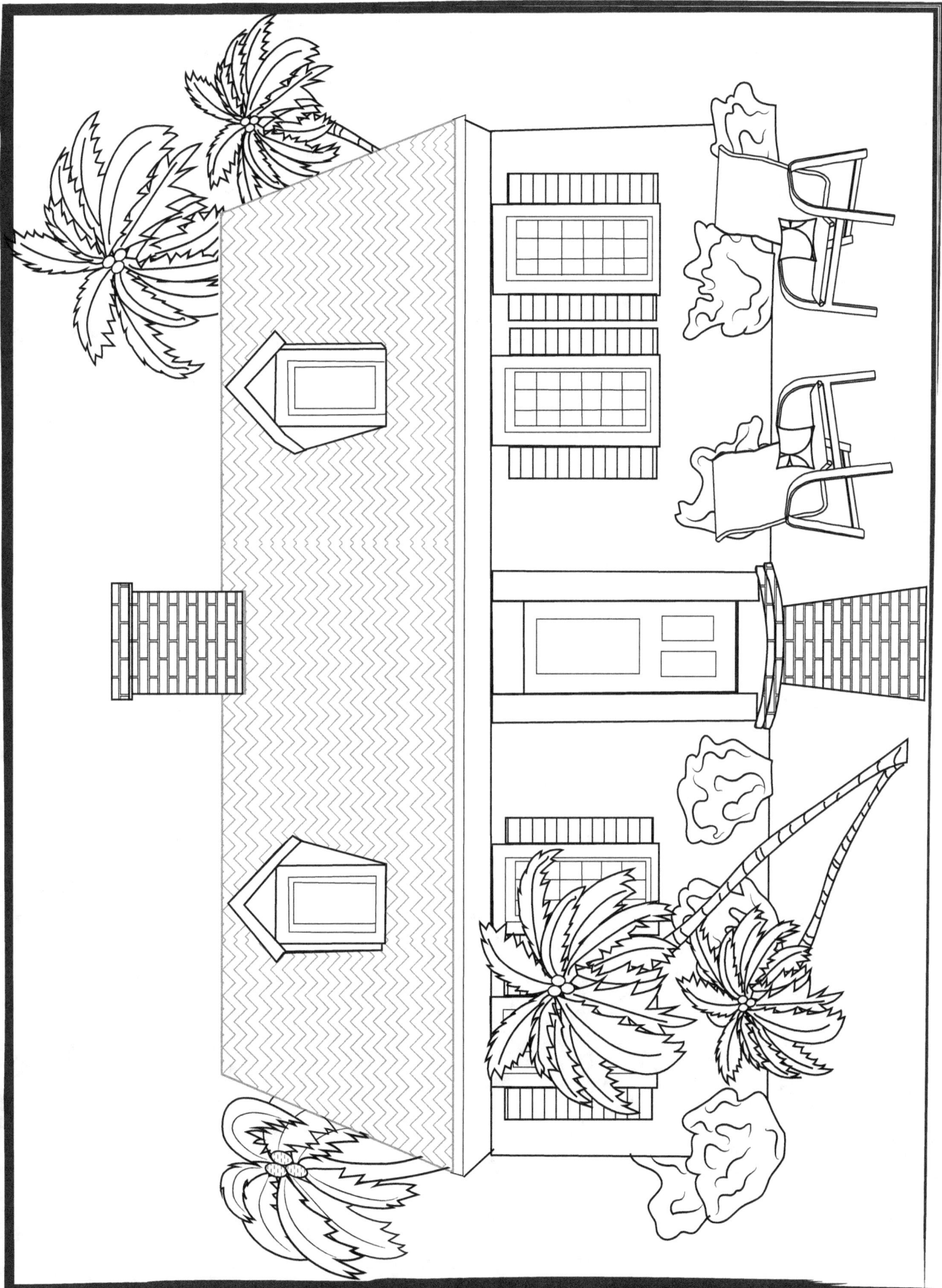

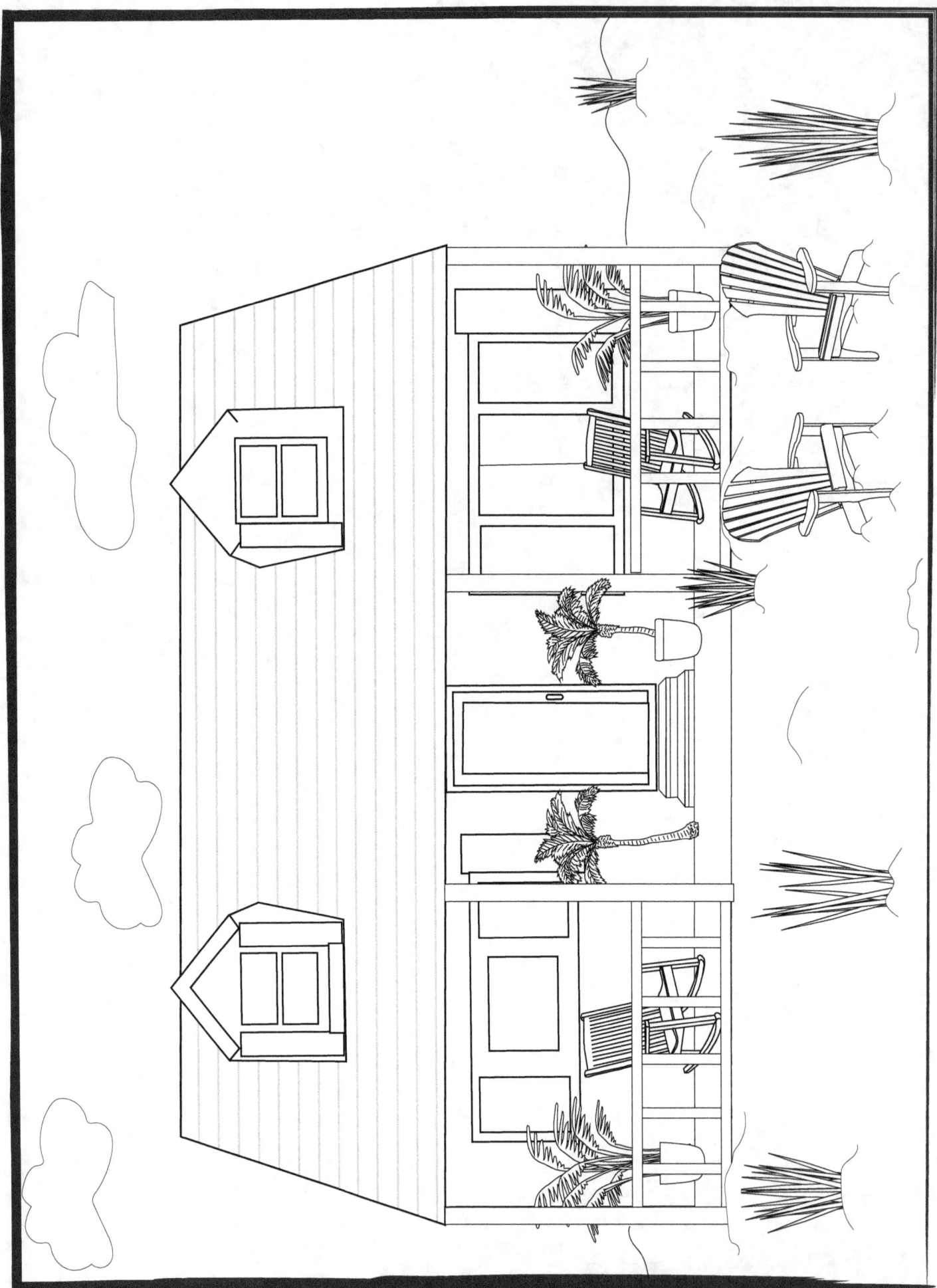

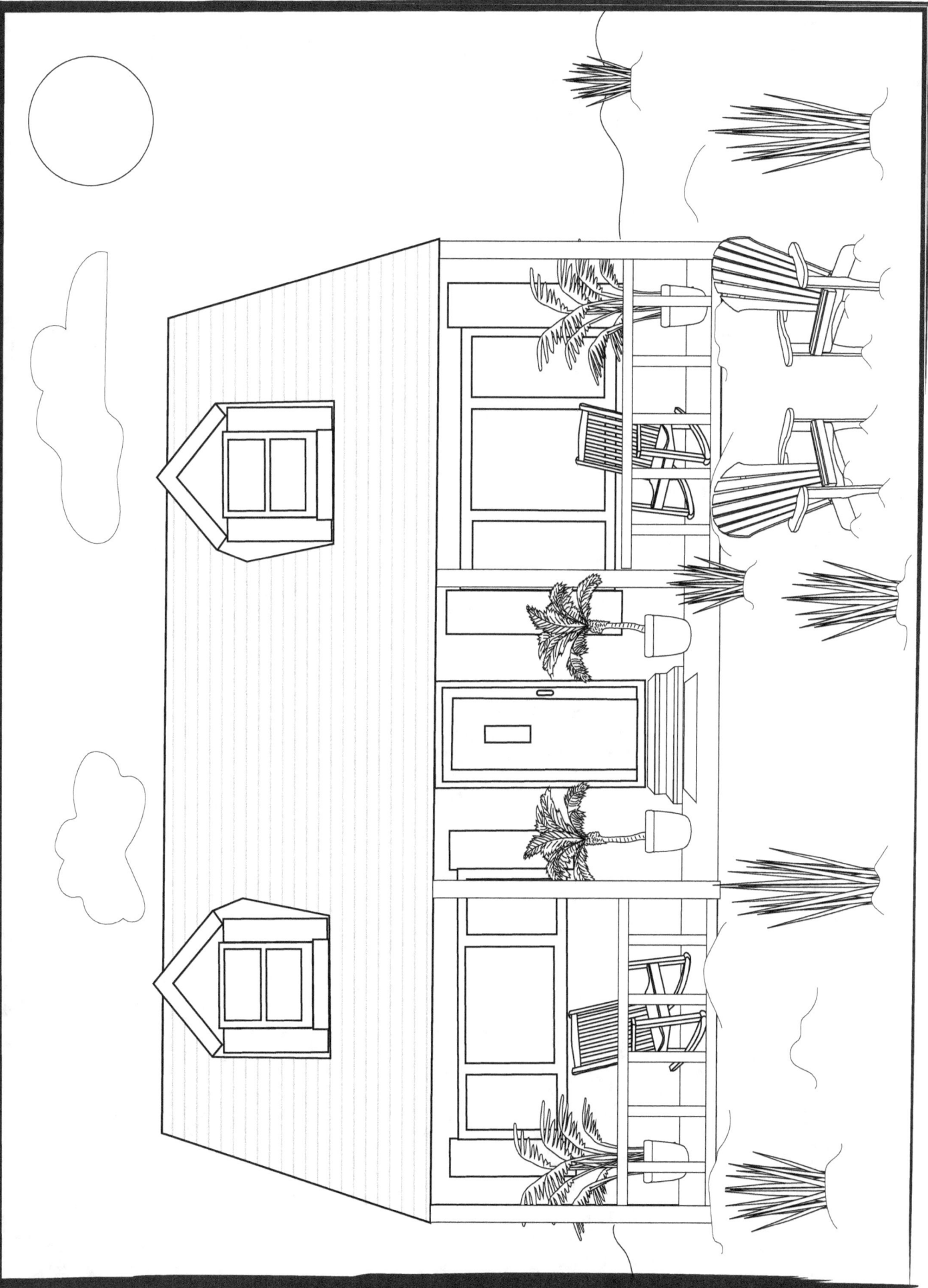

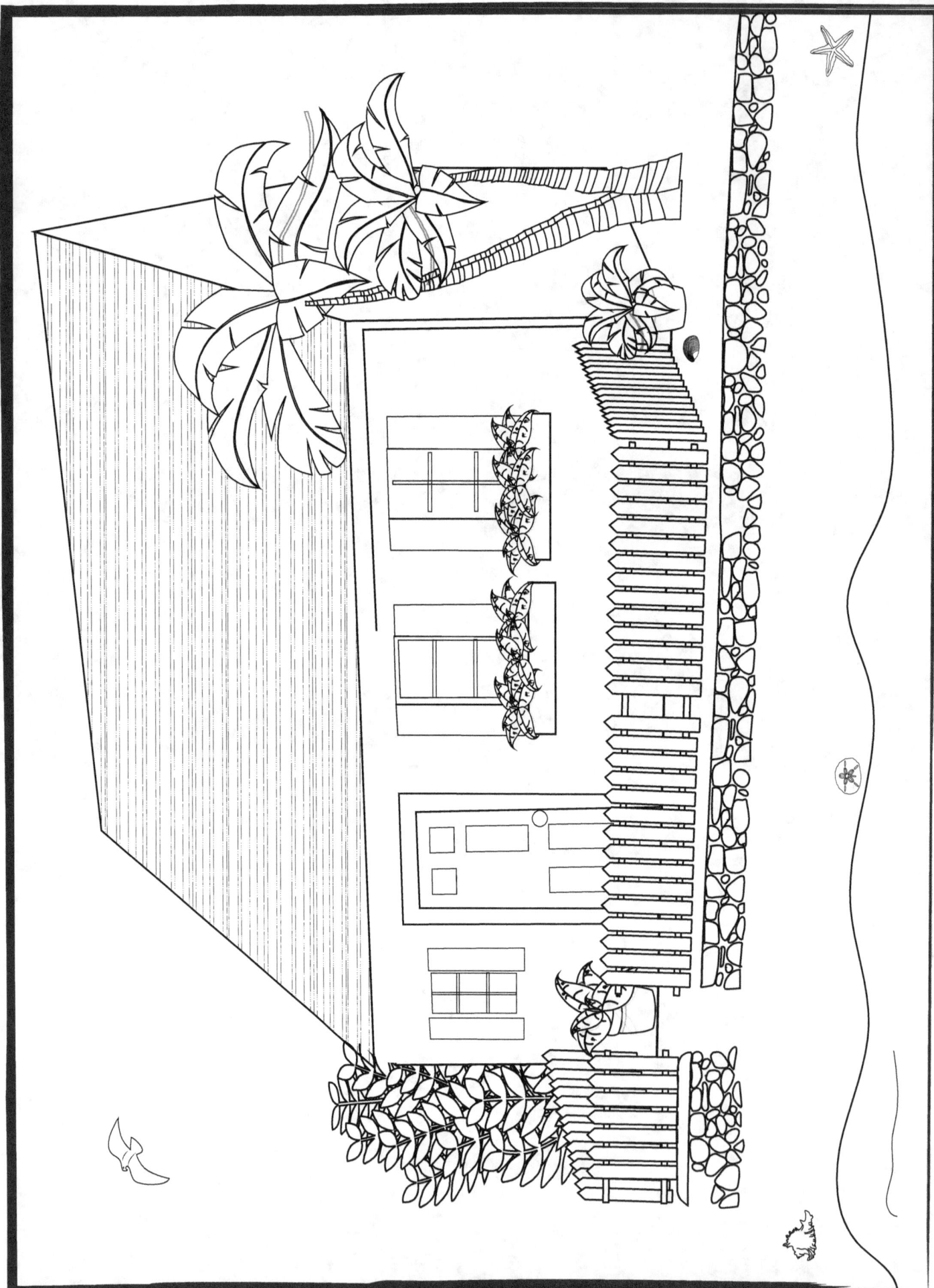

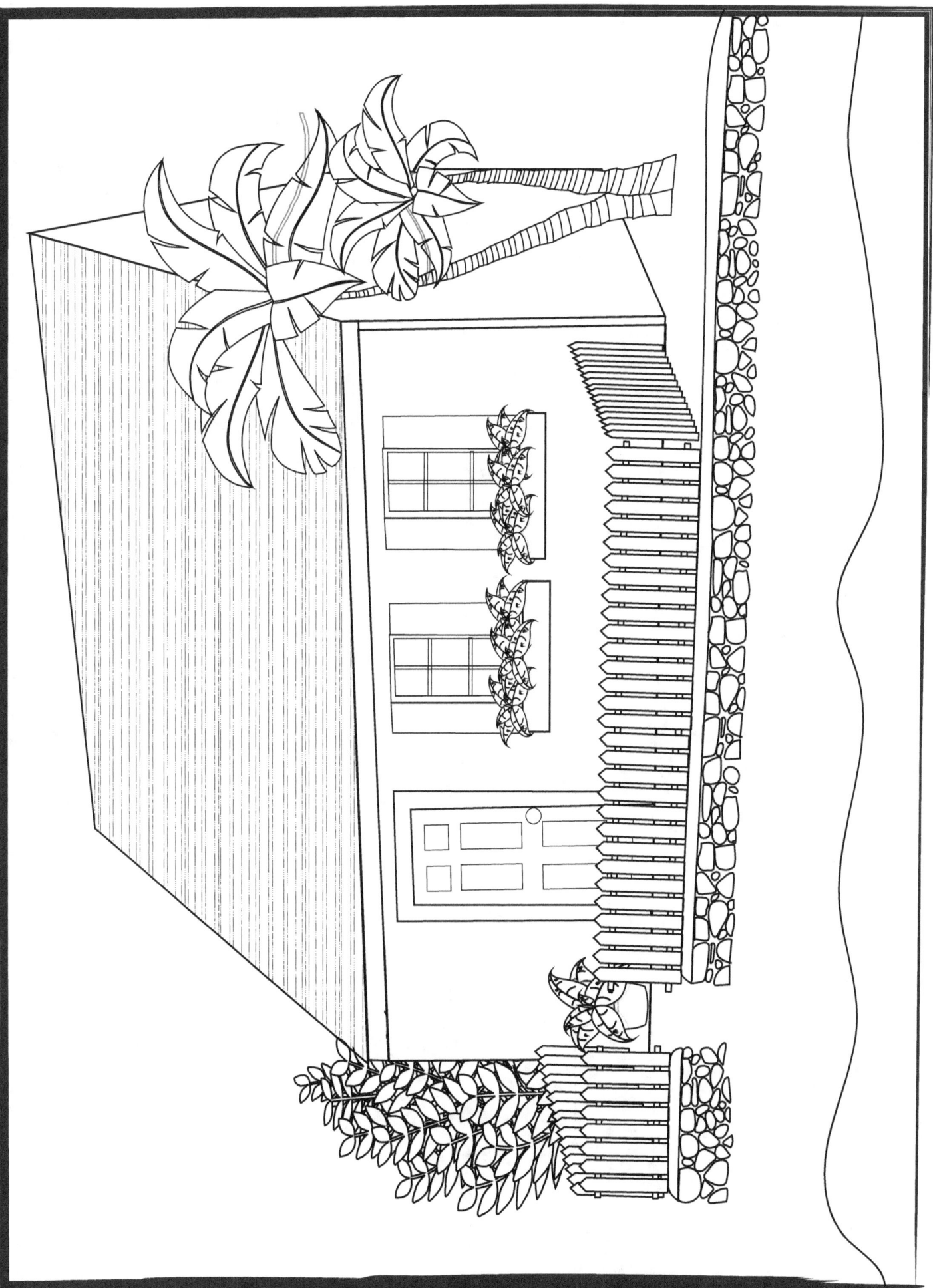

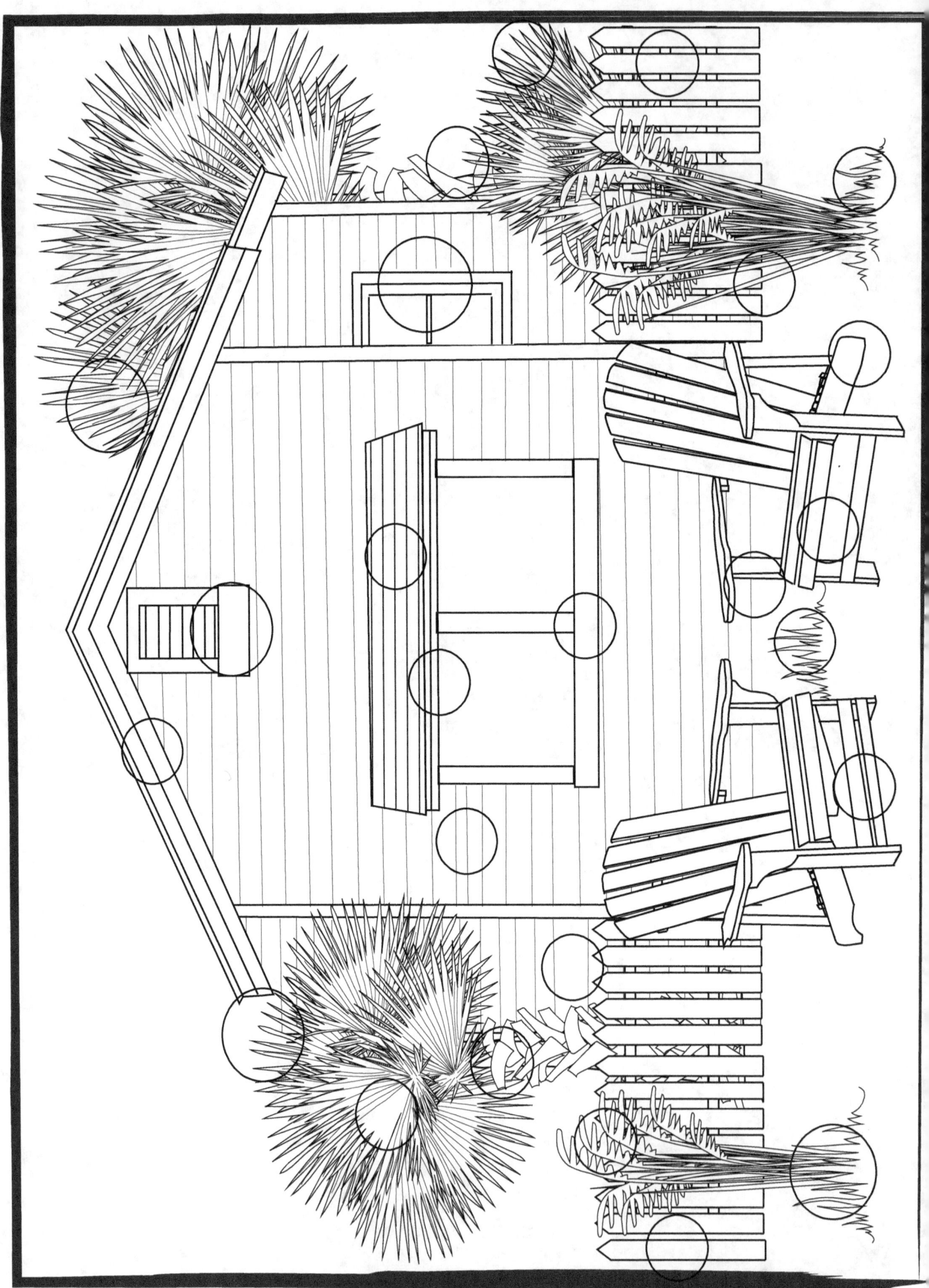

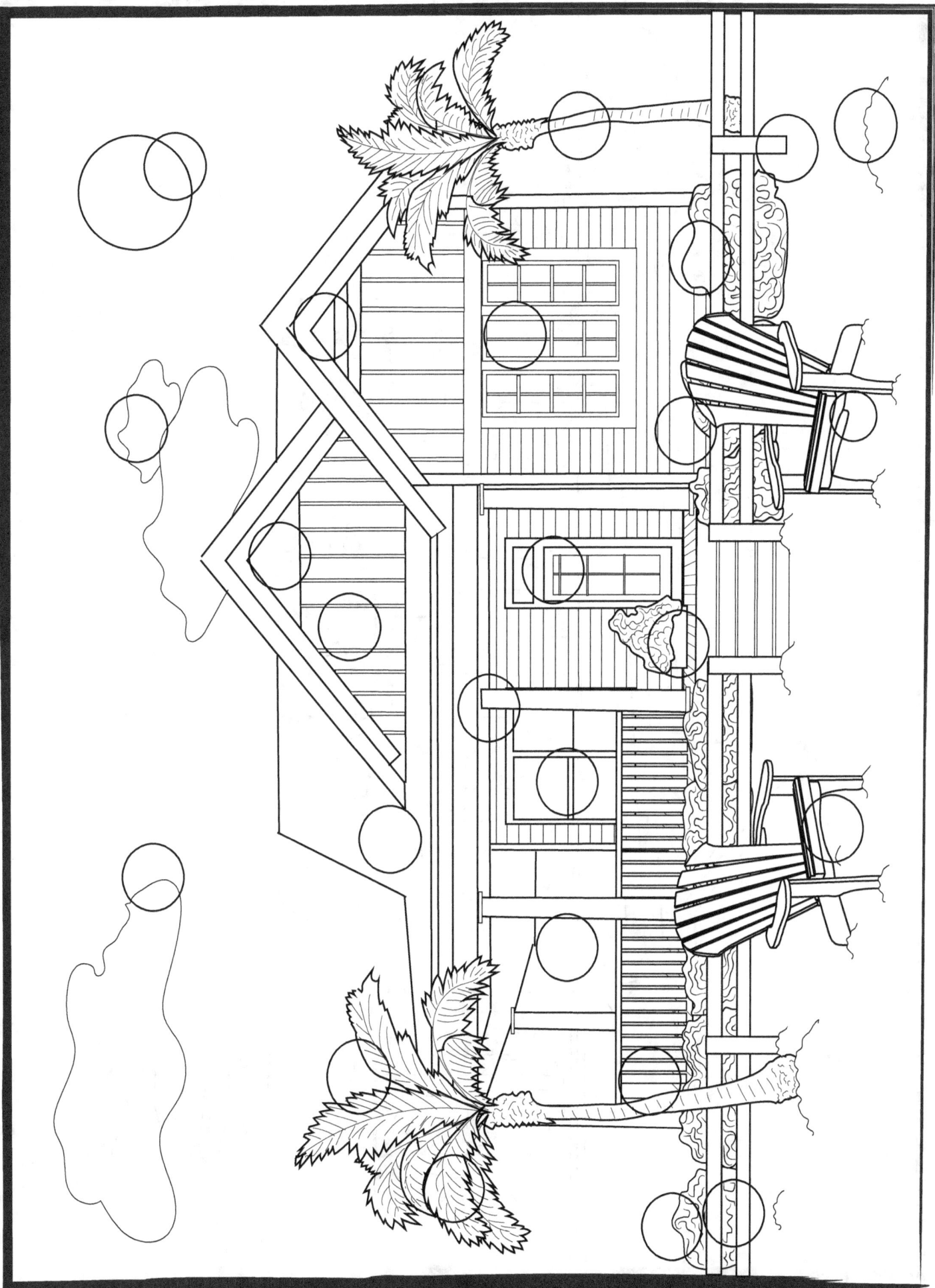

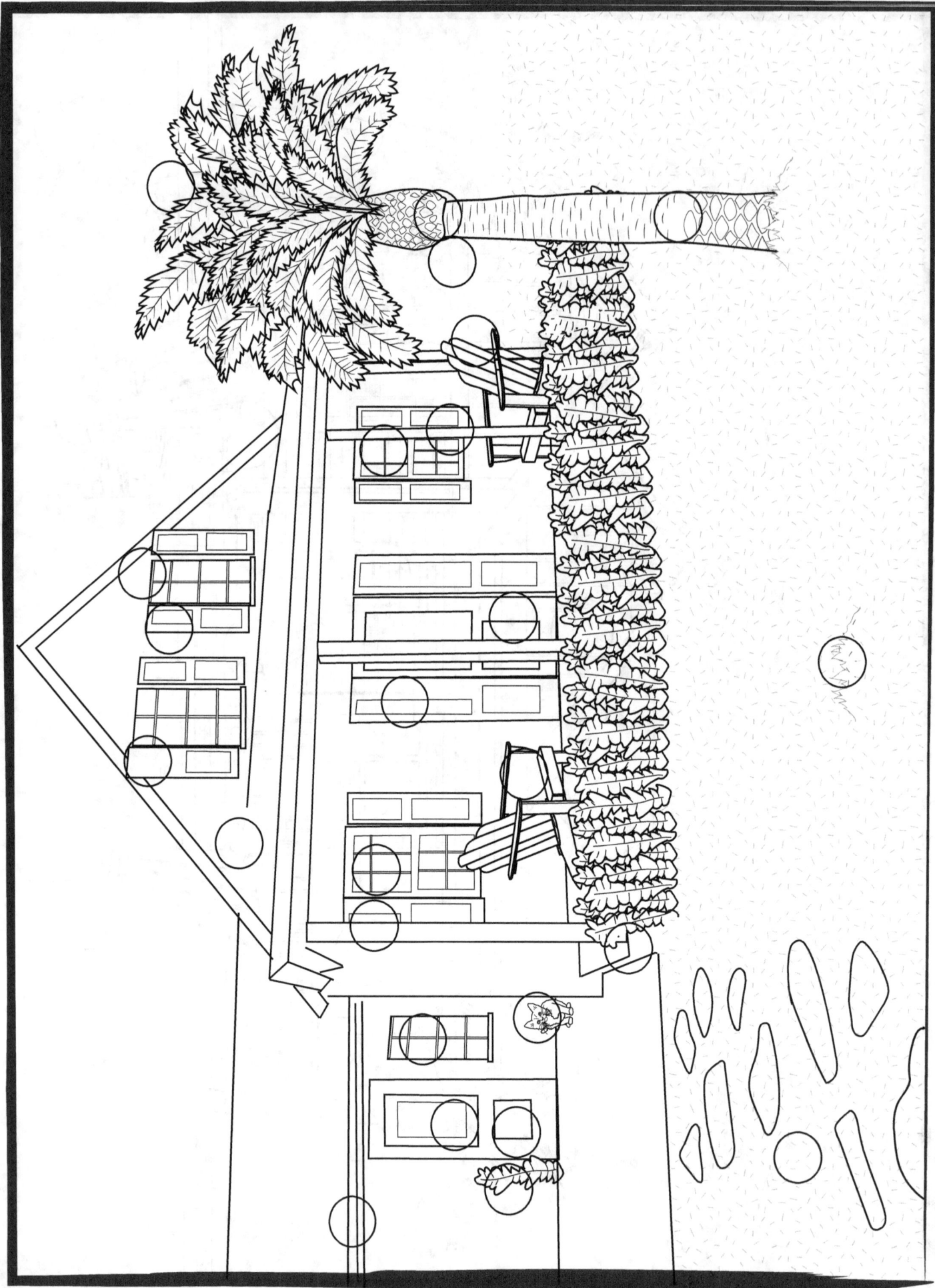

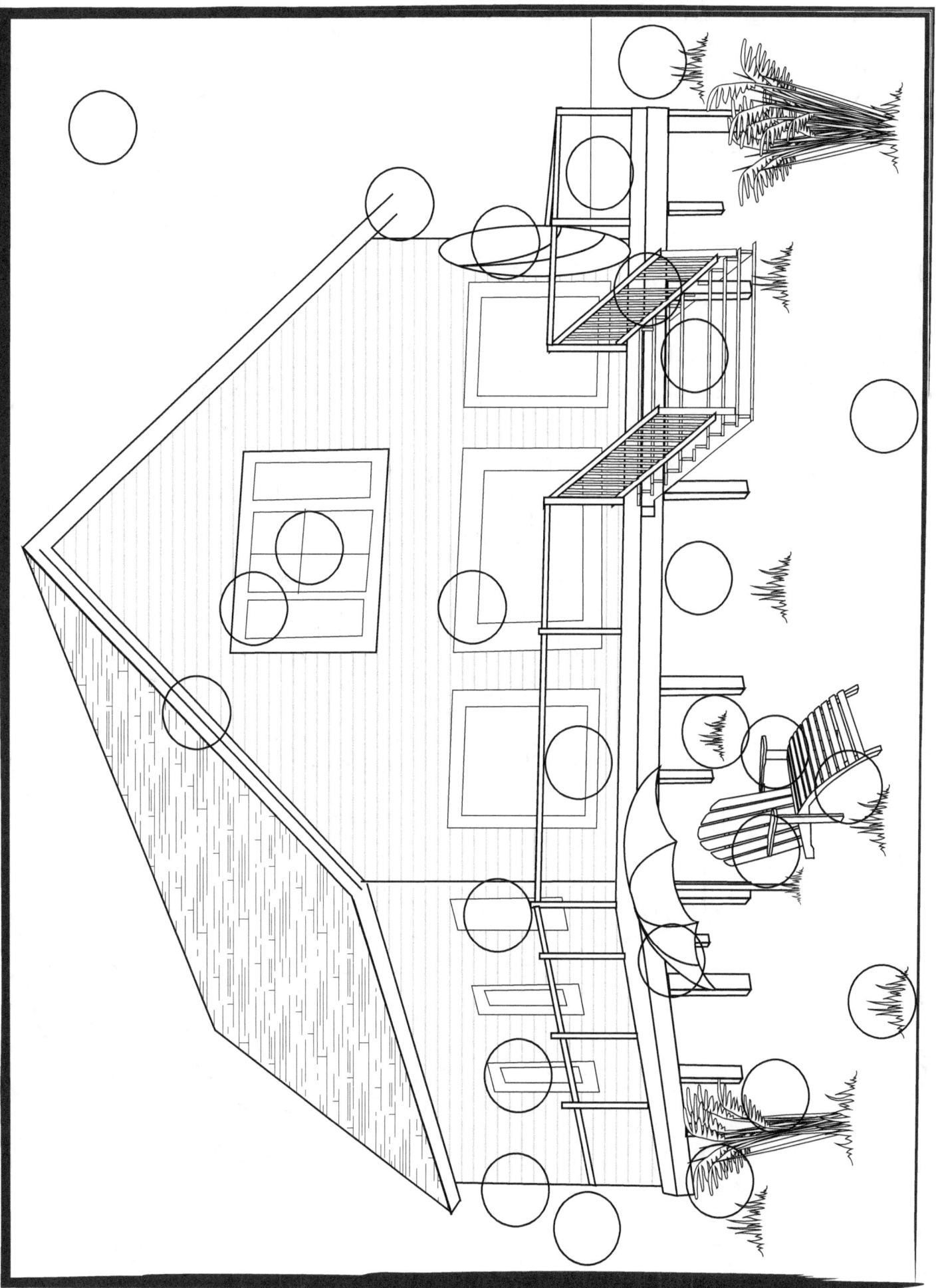

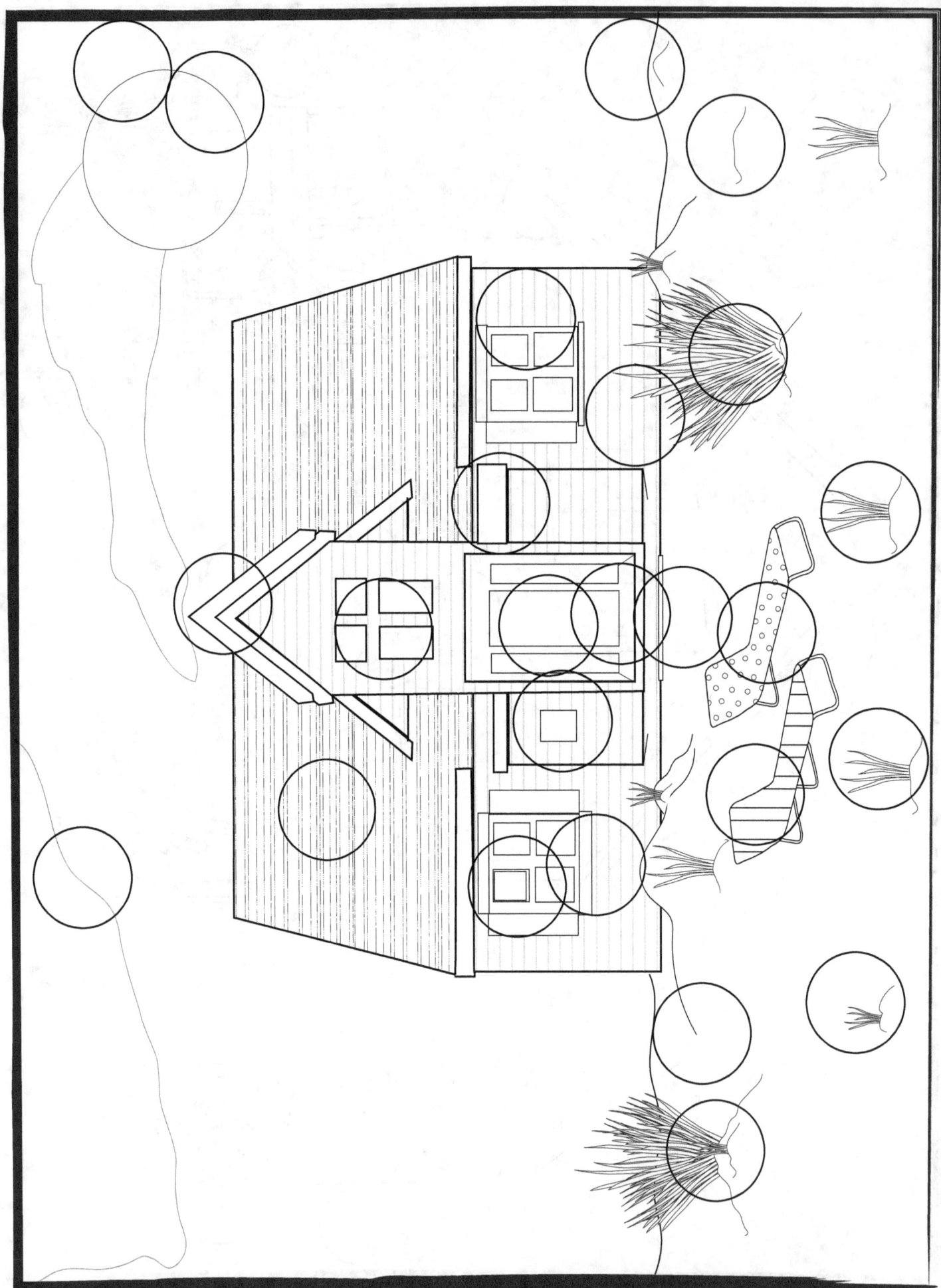

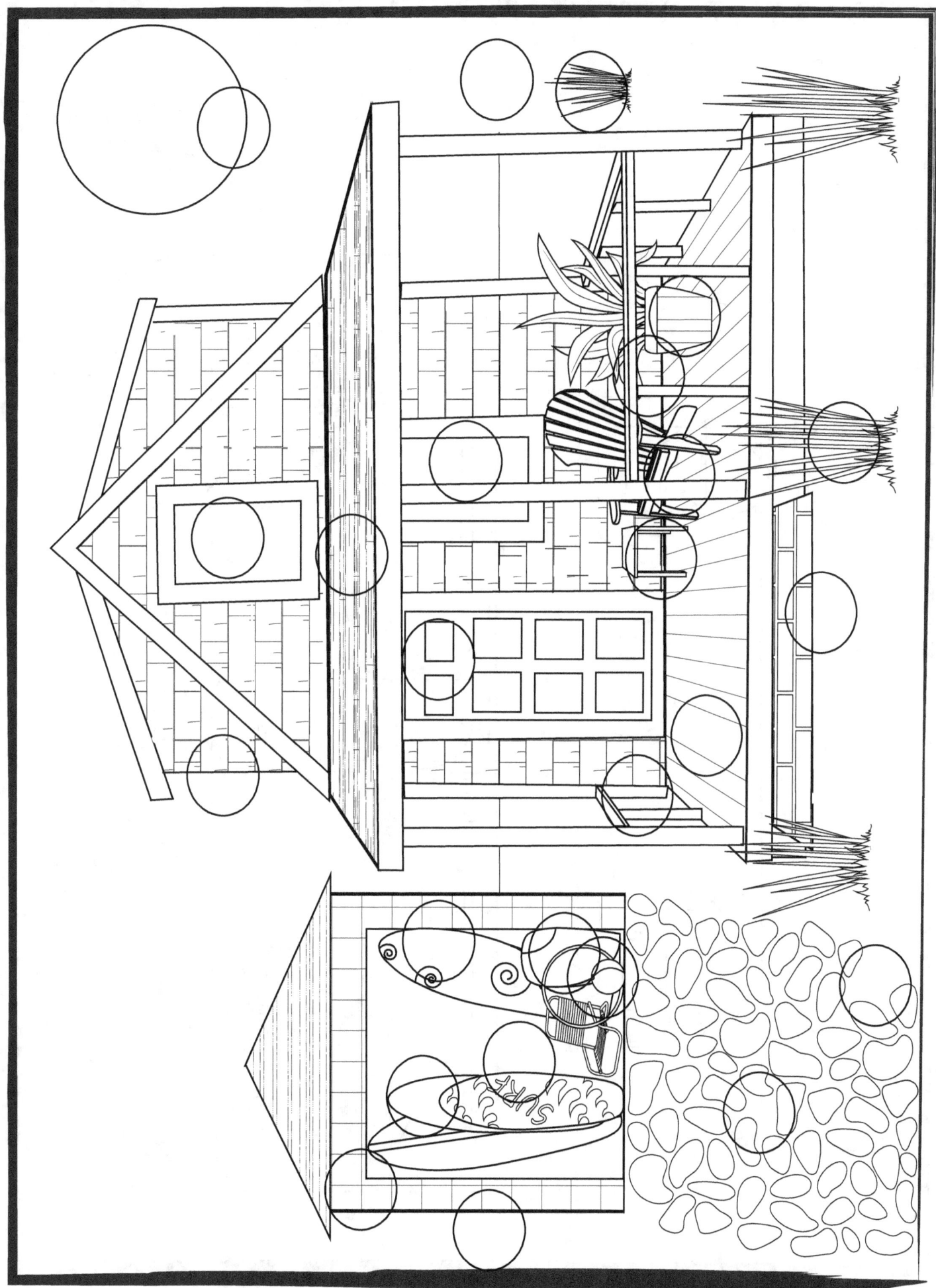

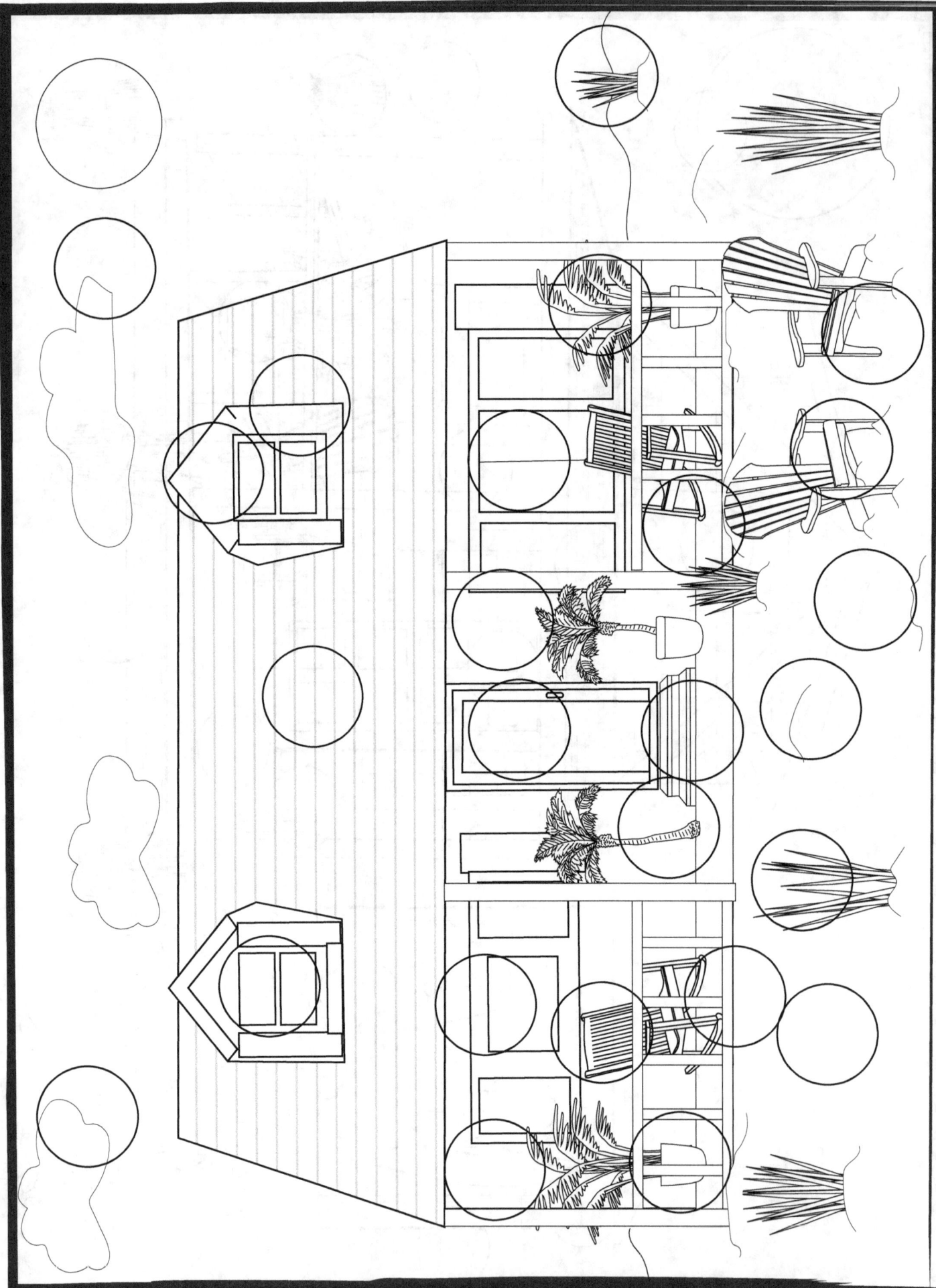

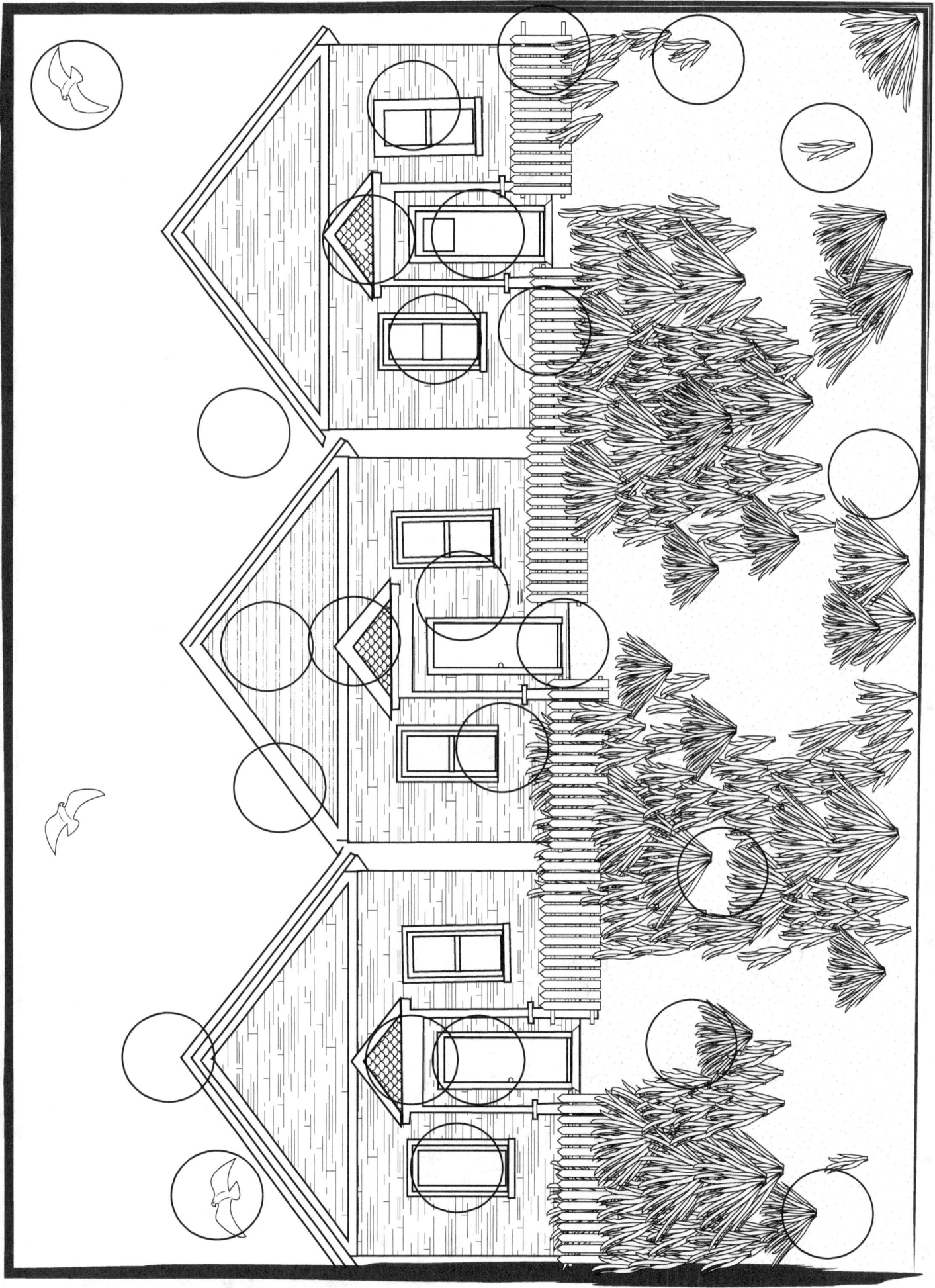

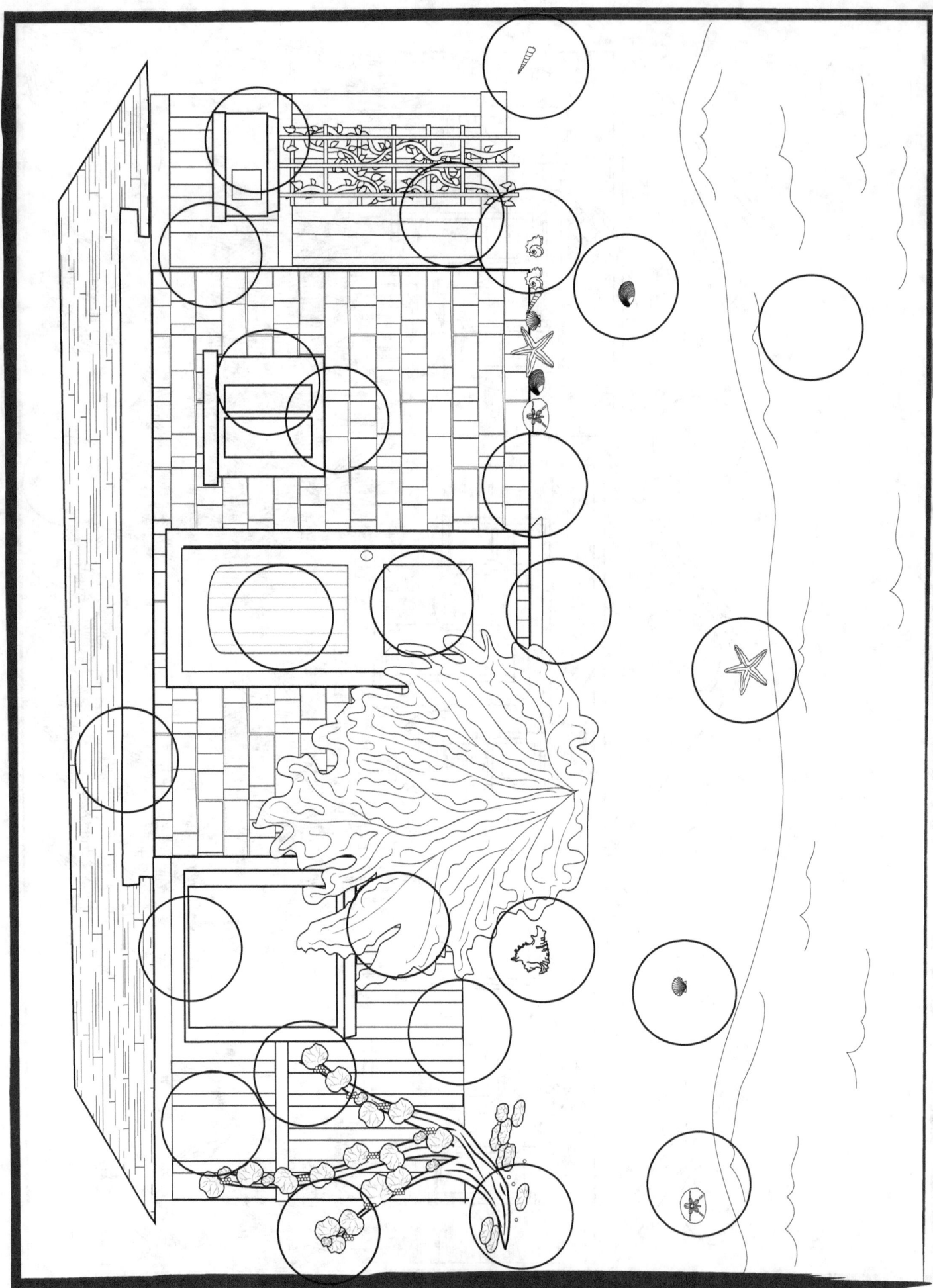

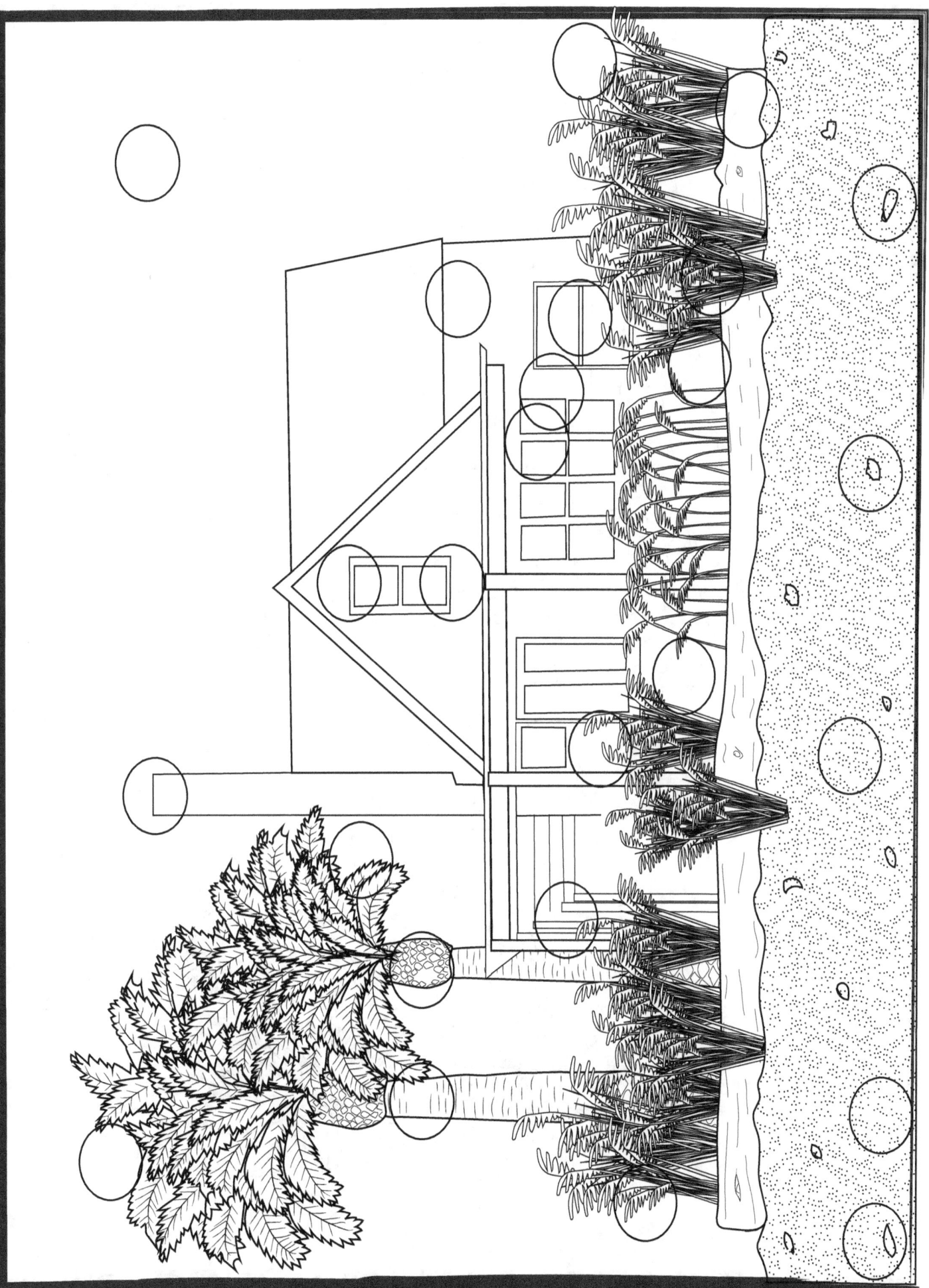

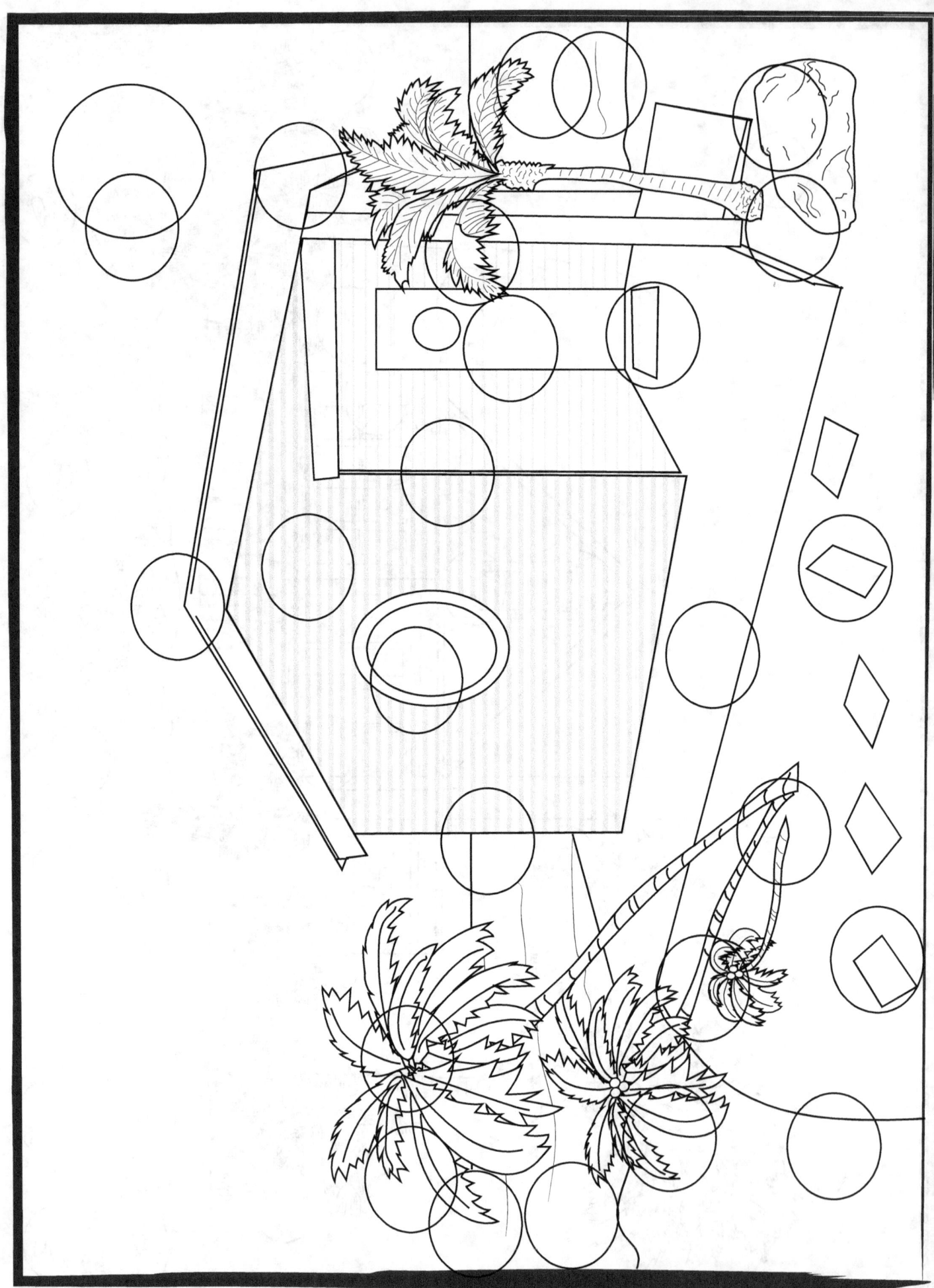

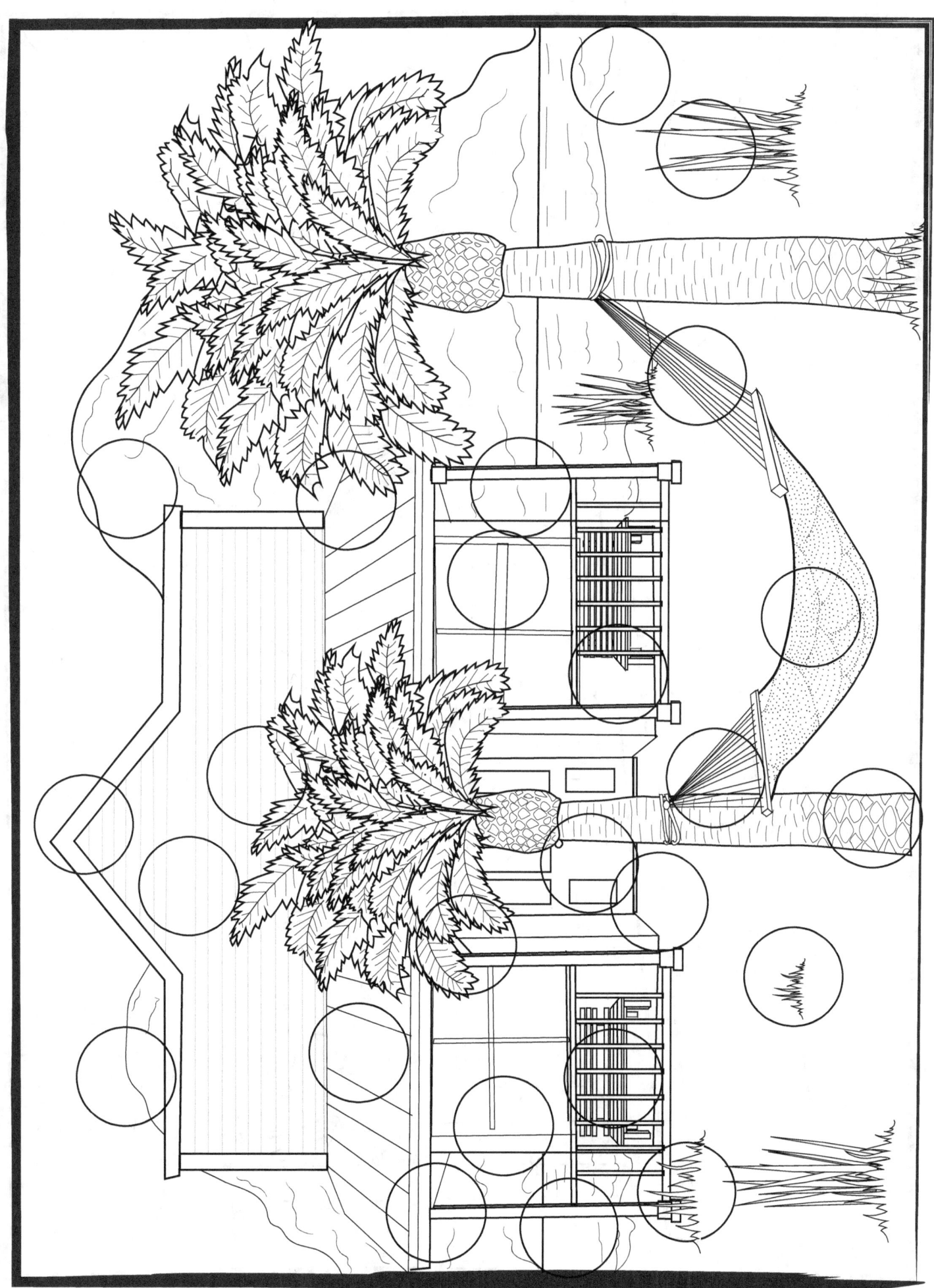

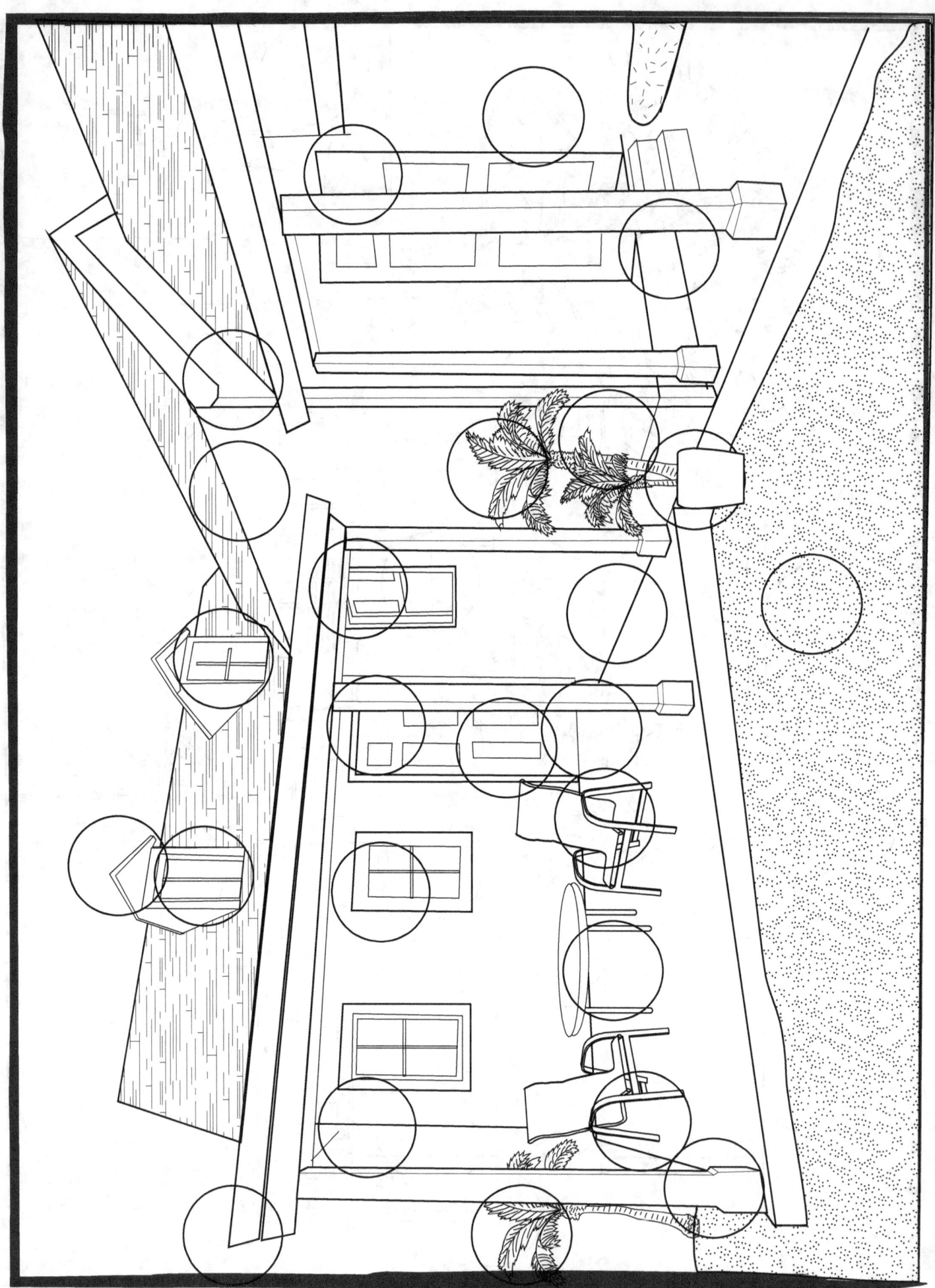

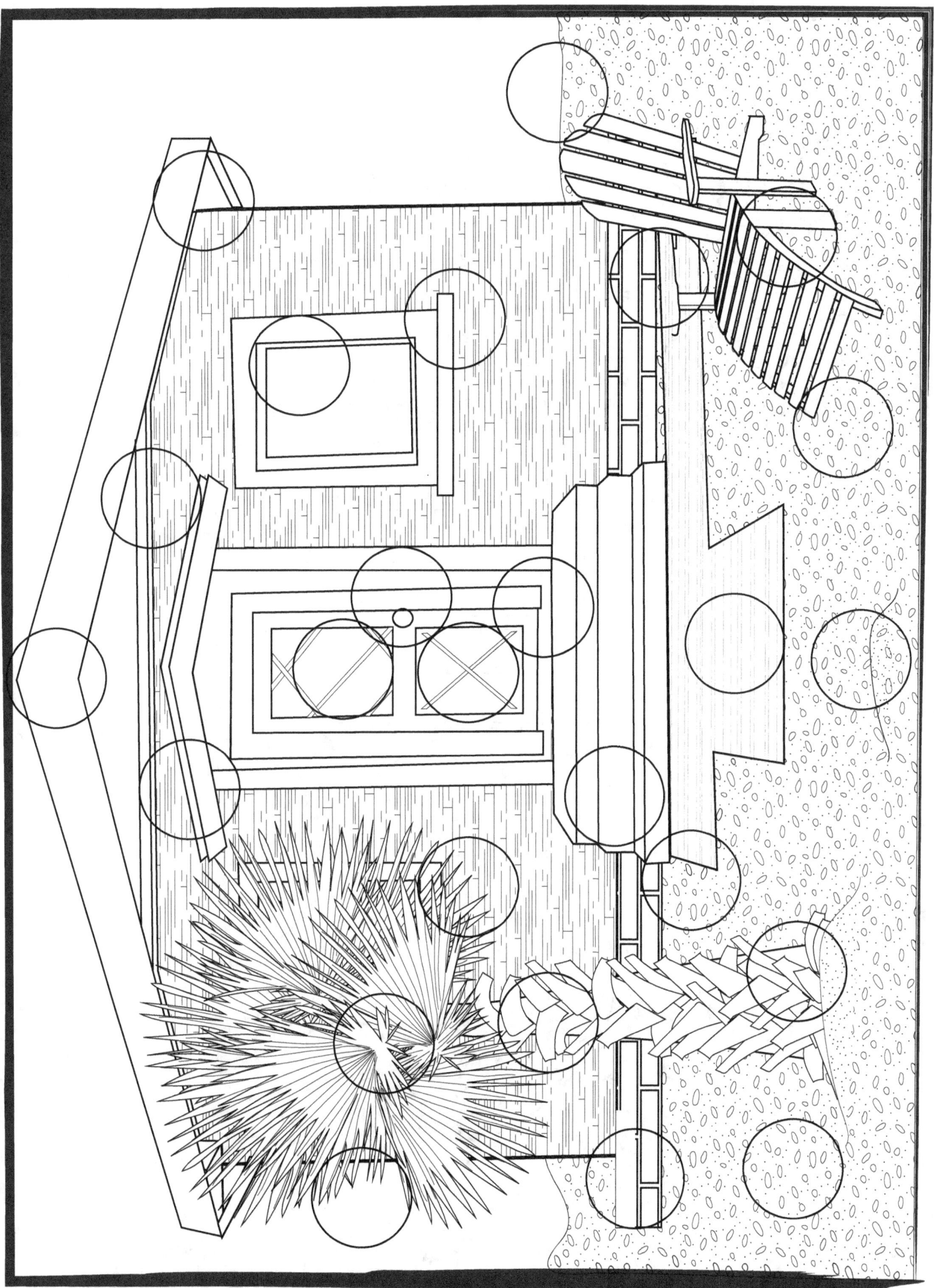

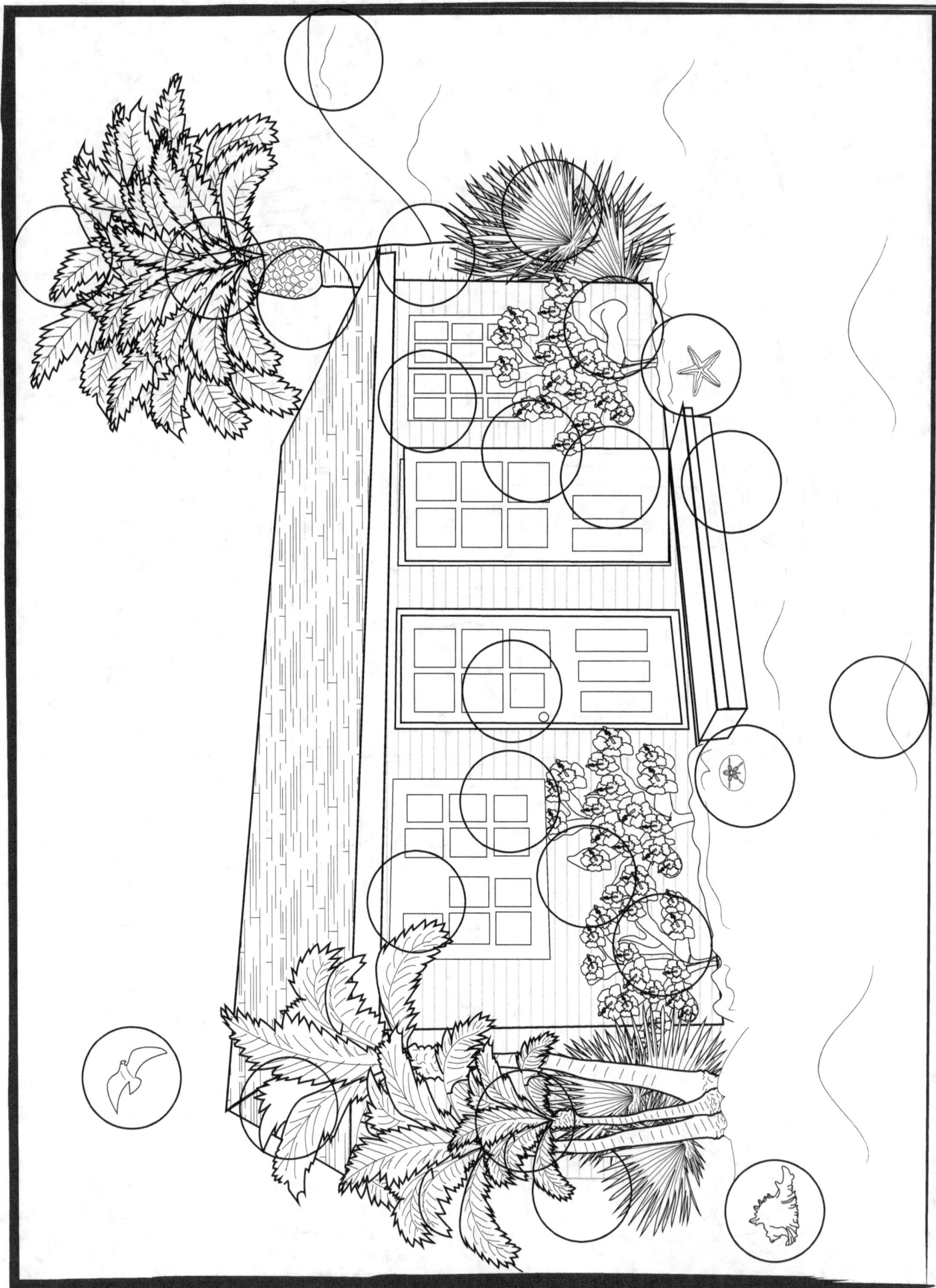

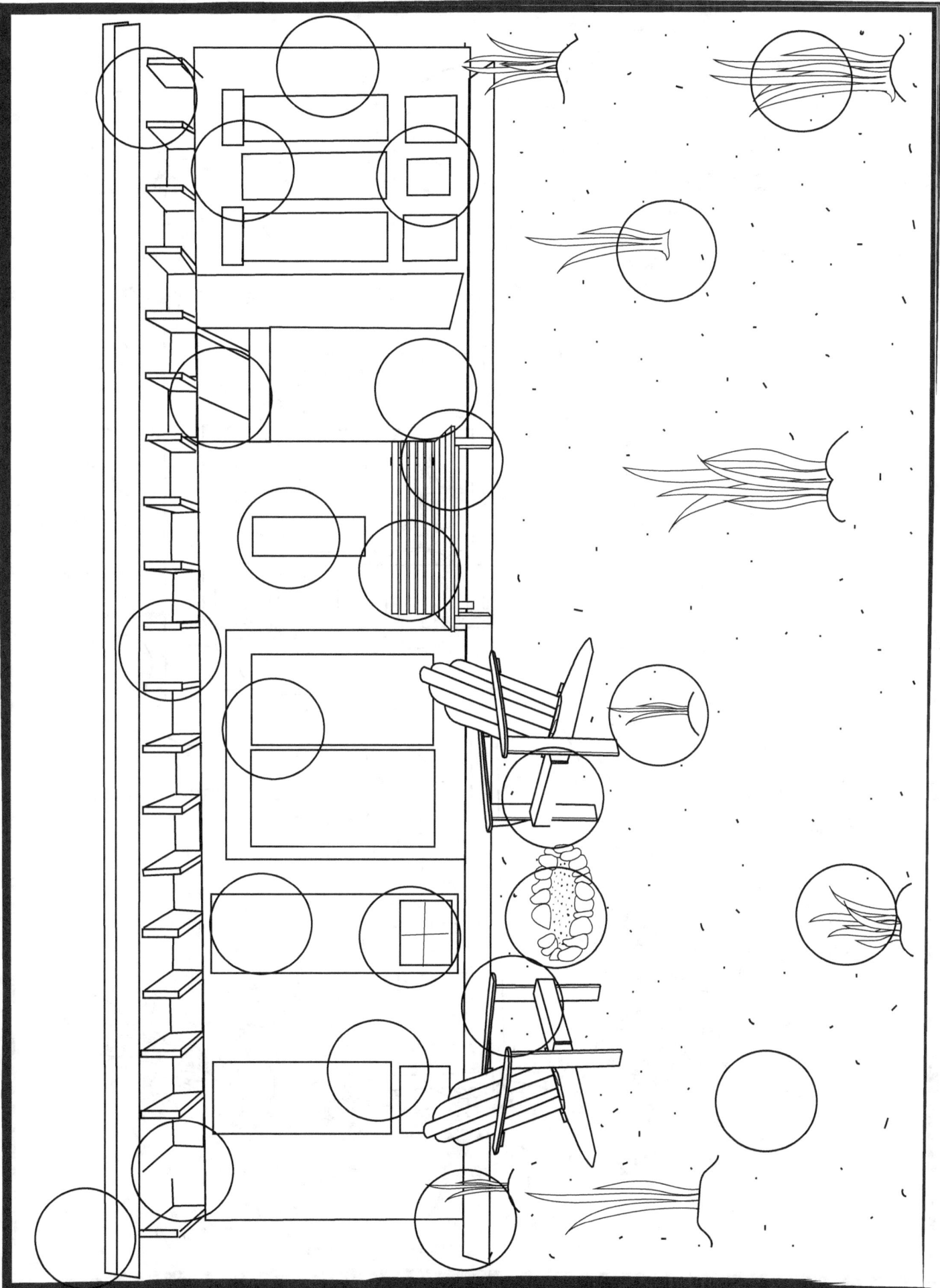

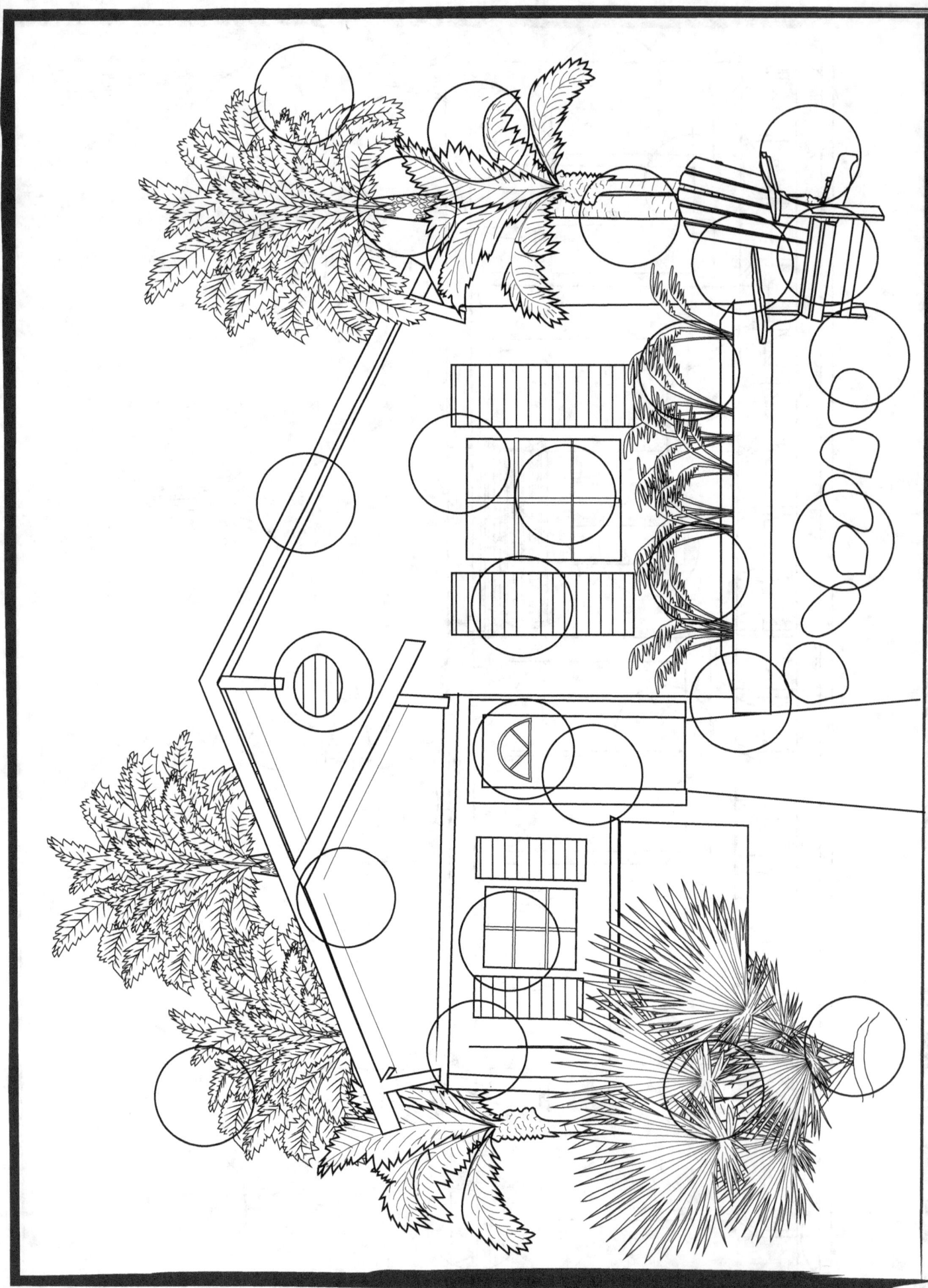

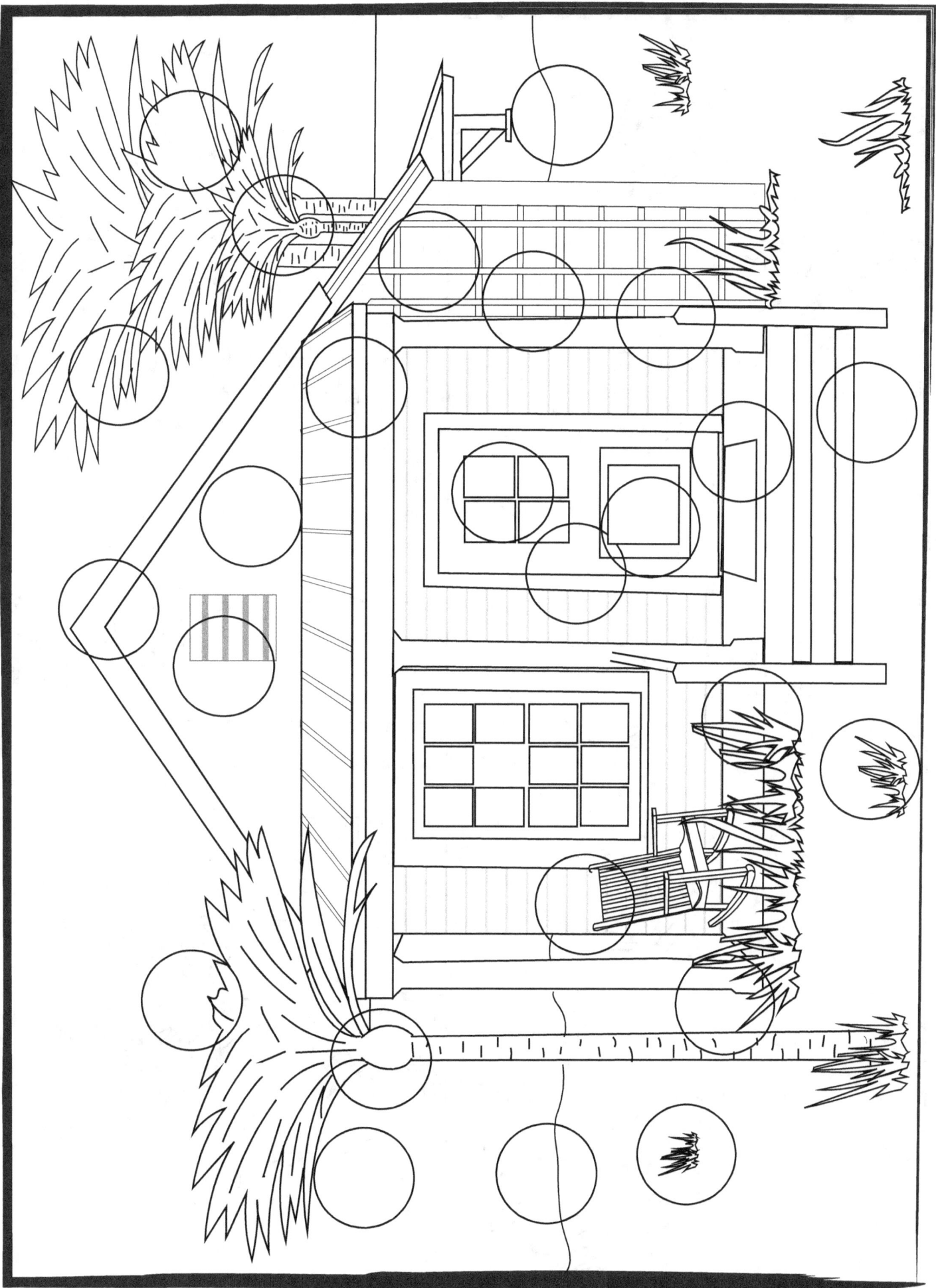

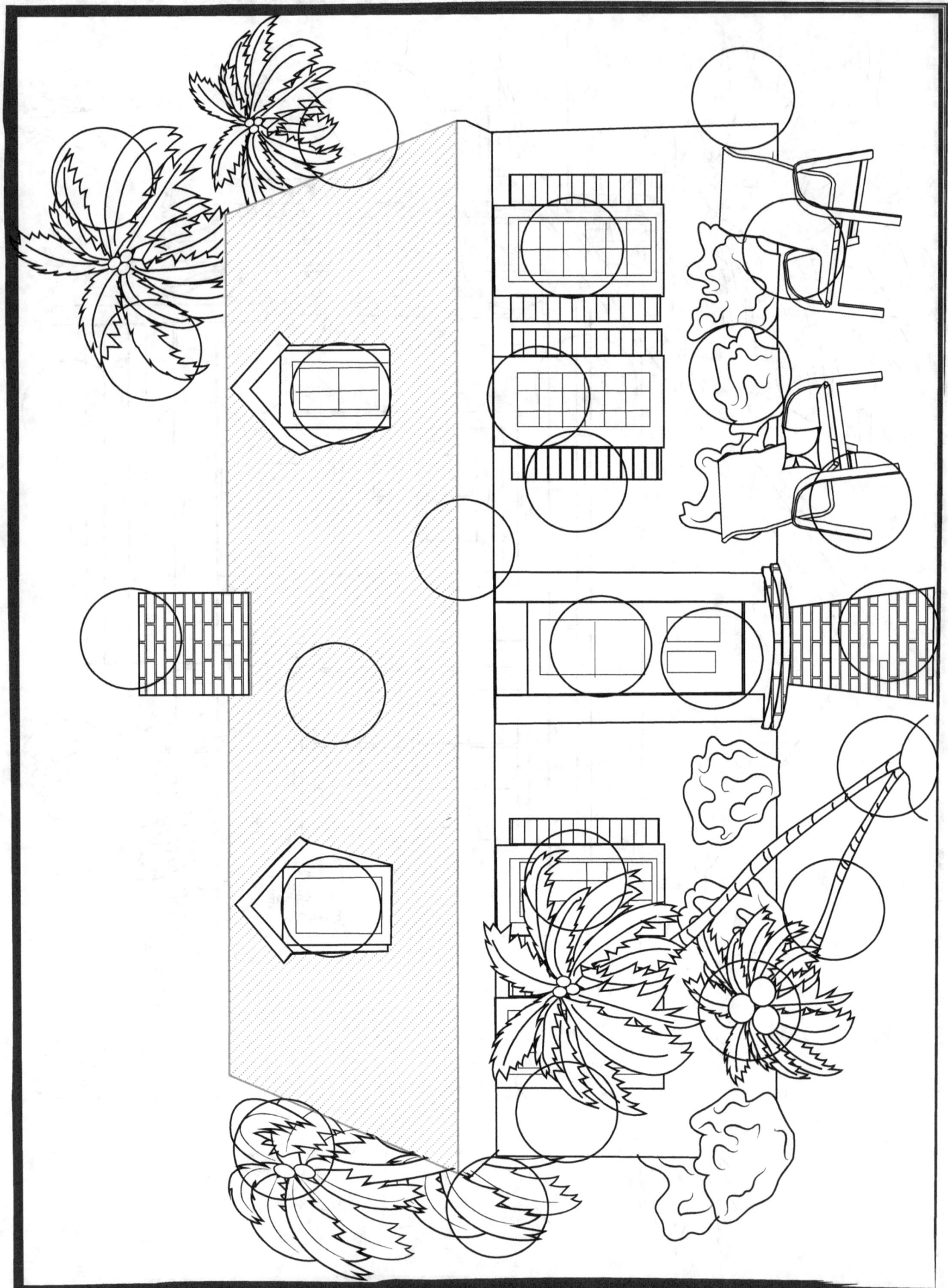

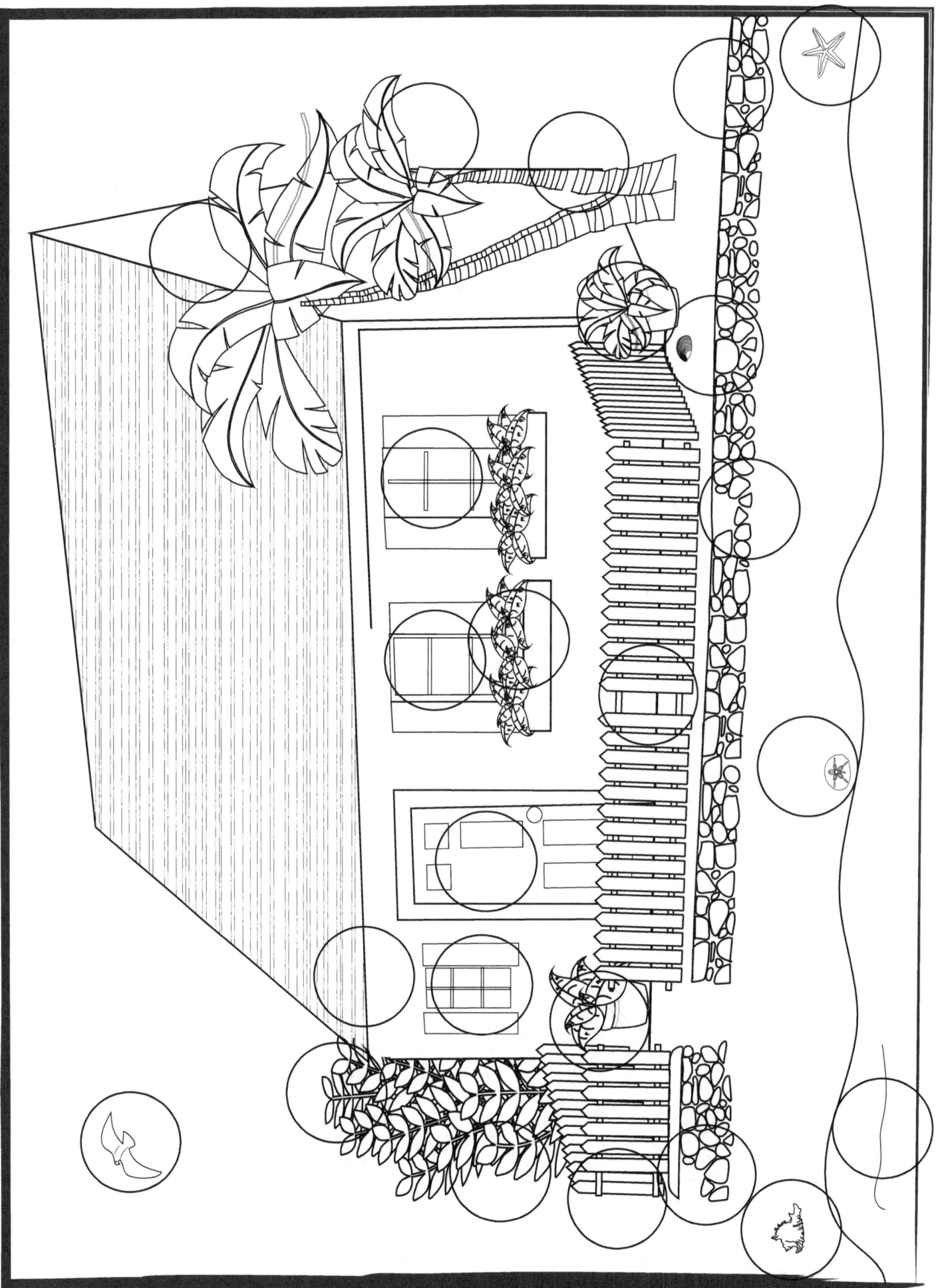